A New Ideology

by

James Nicholls

Copyright © 2015 James Nicholls

jamienicholls1@btinternet.com

All rights reserved, including the right to reproduce this book, or portions thereof in any form. No part of this text may be reproduced, transmitted, downloaded, decompiled, reverse engineered, or stored, in any form or introduced into any information storage and retrieval system, in any form or by any means, whether electronic or mechanical without the express written permission of the author.

ISBN: 978-1-326-28812-9

Foreword

This manuscript is about Distributism and its superiority over Capitalism. In my manifesto I will explain the meaning of Distributism, which I coined as my ideology in politics. The Distributist ideology put forward in this book is not to be misinterpreted as the economic ideology based upon the principles of Catholic social teaching. I will express how the Capitalist world is flawed, and compare Distributism to Capitalism as well as the failures of Communism. The problems facing the world today such as increasing overpopulation, terrorism and economic uncertainty will be addressed as will the explanation for the Distributist solution.

I currently study IB History, which contributes to the verdict on Capitalism and Communism in chapter six. I live in a village in England, somewhat kept away from the busy and polluted areas of modern, urban society. I seemed to of developed the theory of Distributism around the second half of 2014.

By the time you have read this manuscript you will understand the flaws of Capitalism and Communism, and the unrivalled benefits of Distributism. You will see the world in a new light, and you will understand that the world would be a much better place under Distributist rule. Eight chapters and a conclusion are configured whom encompass all different views of Distributist ideology, from foreign affairs, religion, war, economics, population, global warming, culture, laws and order and a general glimpse of what future could look like under a Distributist government.

Be prepared to be dazzled and bewildered by the unique ideologies put forward in the novel and think about what might come of the world under Distributist rule. Many who read this will wonder why it hadn't of been thought of before, and this book will no doubt be completely different to any other political ideology put forward before.

Chapter 1

Muslims, Religion, Terrorists and the EU

I strongly believe that the United Kingdom as a country should rely less on the European Union, the EU threatens UK sovereignty along with all other EU members. The EU is run by unelected politicians out of the public eye, making all the pathetic laws in Brussels. Some believe that the EU was actually a secret Nazi idea in which they would establish if they lost the Second World War, in which Germany and France, run by Nazis would establish and distribute a union, in which Germany would lead and dictate. This myth does explain to an extent why Germany emerged as the leading power of Europe so suddenly after WW2, especially after the UK joined the EU in 1973. If Hitler had a time machine and witnessed today, he would likely be quite happy, given that Germany is the leading power of Europe. Of course, he would be less satisfied that the Jews and many people of all different ethnic groups, especially Asians, have been immigrating to Europe. The other myth is that the EU was actually a Soviet idea, used to secretly establish a Communist union.

Despite the EU promising greater trade and economic aid by being a member, some member states still have weak and fragile growing economies. I strongly dislike how the EU keeps on opening borders up to immigrants, with most of them coming to the UK. EU politicians are naive enough to think that immigrants will help the economy because they will find jobs. However a lot of immigrants that come to the UK don't work, they come here and live on the benefits, taking advantage of the free healthcare system. They live in poverty, some having 10 people living in a small apartment. Most of the immigrants come from the Middle East and India, which explains why they come to the UK to live this lifestyle.

India is vastly overpopulated with most people living in extreme poverty. According to some people it is filthy with rubbish everywhere as well as having a horrid stench. The people from India must come to the UK and think their living in paradise, which they are compared to India. There are rivers and lakes in the Far East, for example that are literally filled with rubbish; you would think it was a dump. Examples would be the Buriganga River in Bangladesh, the Citarum River in Indonesia, the Yellow River in China and the Ganges River in India. Though the East isn't entirely to blame, pollution is spreading to the west as well due to the rapid overpopulation caused by industrialisation in the previous centuries. To be honest, I don't think India should have become independent; it would have been better off under British rule.

Muslims are another threat that the UK has to deal with, which the EU has only made worse by encouraging immigrants largely from the Middle East. The young Muslims, under the influence of the Islamic State are the main threat. Their poisoned minds could and probably will lead to suicide bombers in built up areas in the near future, where there is the potential risk of them taking thousands of lives. All the Muslims, in my opinion, should just go back to where they came from as it will benefit Britain's sovereignty as a European country and the country will be much safer without terrorists roaming around cities.

Britain wasn't where they came from, why should our nation help foreign people when most of them do nothing to help our society? In the future they will come here when their countries are vastly overpopulated, taking our resources and the state having to feed them, then they'll reproduce like rats and send our country into famine where millions will perish. They live and thrive off the benefits and because many Muslim families have many children, combined with the ever increasing number of immigrants, the countries native white people will eventually be outnumbered by Muslim fanatics. What if a Muslim political party rises up and seizes power or if there is a revolution? The more Muslims in the country the more likely it will become, with Terrorism propaganda at its maximum, the future generation of British Muslims who have been born in Britain, won't be 'British' at all, they will stick to their culture and eventually once their numbers increase, there will be a national revolution. Now the revolution could be extremely bad for the unfortunate western British people, if terrorists seize power like I said before, they could make Islam compulsory; make it an Islamic dictatorship in which anyone deemed unfaithful in Allah will be executed.

Muslims have an obsessive belief in the Quran, in a book which contains verses which contradict each other. The first part of the book teaches about peace, while the second half teaches about the killing of non-Muslims. The religion also exploits women and mercifully slaughter innocent animals. The prophet Mohammad was actually a selfish, God-fearing person, he had multiple wives and killed many innocent people. Nearly every terrorist in 2015 has faith in Islam, which promotes the fact that Islam itself is not a peaceful religion. Islam also condemns masturbation, which is probably why there are high reports of rape in the Middle East. Another thing that deeply annoys me is when Muslim women wear burqa's, or veils. For one I find it quite rude when a person hides their face and also because wearing burqa's has never been part of British culture historically. Britain has always been inhabited with a majority of white people, and it should remain that way, otherwise the world may as well be united under one country. Muslim women who wear burqa's should at least have their veils torn off their faces and dumped.

In schools recently, the English educational system has begun to indoctrinate young children by encouraging them to fully mingle with Muslims and to encourage new mosques in the UK. This educational indoctrination, likely spread by Muslim and non-British teachers, will ultimately make the next generation Islam and immigration friendly. Unless something is done about this, the UK will cease to be British; becoming culturally ruined over the next century as a result of friendly immigration which will encourage immigrants to abandon British culture and stick to their own which will make the UK more diverse than ever.

Despite their being a number of immigrants coming to Europe, most go to France and the UK, Germany meanwhile gets off lightly. Perhaps the Nazis did win the Second World War in the long term, by defeating the rest of Europe economically and culturally ruining France and Britain by encouraging immigration. The other problem of the EU is that it prevents decisive government, things take months to negotiate, and David Cameron has to go to the German Chancellor (Coincidence?) Angela Merkel to discuss policies and everything. Going to the Queen is bad enough, but having to have the German approval makes a decisive government in the realms of fantasy. A country with such a prestige as ours should be fully independent and we aren't. We will never be fully independent unless we come out of the EU. It is likely they will still trade with us, the EU sanctioning us for leaving would be ridiculous, we still have a high influence on the European market and by not trading with us, all EU members will lose something. We shouldn't have to help other EU members out as well as we are struggling as it is. Whatever the EU's true motives are, it is at present ruining parts of Europe and will continue to do so.

We aren't exactly in the Muslims good books as we helped the Americans against terrorism. There is no doubt many Muslims under the influence of terrorist groups who hate the British; we're probably number 2 on their list of the countries they hate the most, behind the USA. If the terrorists developed nuclear weapons in the future, the Americans and us will suffer the brunt of it. The Muslim population is rising quite rapidly too, and if one Islamic extremist ever takes leadership of a country, the freedom to choose your religion would be curtailed. Islamic extremists also believe that anyone who stops being a Muslim, should be executed. That is why it is vital to eradicate the Muslim population from the UK unless one wants to have Islam as a compulsory religion.

Therefore it is necessary to ban Muslim as a religion in the state whilst people practicing the Buddhist, Christianity, Atheist and Spirituality religions should be supported. My own religious theories is that God is a mystical energy, which created space, the Big Bang and science itself. This energy (God) created the Big Bang and is still going around the universe creating new planets. This theory explains science and it explains where the Big Bang came from. Adding on to that theory, the energy is merely a deity, so praying to God will not bring any results because the mystical energy isn't actually a living thing, but rather a force. The mystical energy goes round the universe and opens up Black Holes, for the reason why Black Holes are formed is unclear. Perhaps 'God' creates the Black Hole's to eradicate advanced civilisations, as superior civilisations will eventually go out to conquer other planets, thus creating Black Hole's would be necessary by God to exterminate advanced civilisations before they become too advanced and prevent life development on other planets.

My other theory is that the Black Hole's, actually eat up all planets and stars at the same point in time, like an Armageddon scenario. After the universe is swallowed, then 'White Holes' manifest, evolving from Black Holes and spitting out all the planets again, 'Time' restarts again therefore with the planets un-inhabitable from the start and eventually evolving to support life. Henceforth, this second theory does establish that the current universe had a beginning, but the White/Black Holes are seemingly eternal and together they collectively create and destroy universes, and then restart over again in a cycle. If this theory is true, then it would also mean that time itself, is only an illusion in a sense that the lifespans of the universes created by the White Hole were all destroyed at the same time, and that everything that takes place within time is supposedly meant to happen. Otherwise, the universe could be controlled by a higher force or life form (God) which continually improves the universe each cycle for its own desires.

In reality, though, there has to be a limit to what science itself can actually achieve and therefore the pinnacle of human technology, a point in time when our technology becomes so advanced, it becomes over-complicated and too mind-blowing even to the top scientists. For the average person for instance, the moon landings and the numerous planets cannot be fully verified, the moon landings and NASA's satellites may just be hoaxes, though unlikely, there is always the possibility. Science itself is limited, as although science attempts to explain the various materials and energies in the universe, they fail to explain where the materials actually came from. Most scientists agree that the Big Bang Theory created our planet, even if it is true, there presumably has to be something that created the Big Bang, Space itself, the laws of physics and science itself. For this reason, science is very much limited in explaining where the actual universe came from, and will eventually cease to become understandable to the human mind.

New religions such as the one I have explained should of course be supported as well. The terrorists in the Middle East should be dealt with swiftly, before they develop nuclear weapons, their first target would likely be the US and the UK. Anyone suspected of being a Muslim in the state should be expelled to eliminate potential terrorism in the future and to protect the sovereignty of the state. Buddhism, Christianity, Spirituality, Atheism, New Religions and other peaceful religions should be supported and protected. Religious rituals of the slaughtering or abuse of animals, however, will not be tolerated and all living animals deserve rights just as much as Humans, in the form of unwanted physical harm

All mosques in the UK should be rightfully demolished, it isn't fair how we open up our borders to thousands of Muslim immigrants and then waste our resources constructing religious buildings to make them happy. These buildings and their own religion, as evidenced from the Islamic State and its use of propaganda on social media, poisons people's minds and pure British people shouldn't be indoctrinated by this monstrous religion, all Muslims MUST be eradicated from UK soil. Muslims drive around in expensive cars, scrounge benefits off the government, indoctrinate children, annoyingly speak Arabic all the time and they are in general, an impulsive culture.

Muslims and immigrants alike were also mostly responsible for the 2011 riots which was ignited when police rightfully shot Mark Duggan who was thought to be planning a terrorist attack. A long civil war between the immigrants and human rights activists and

British people could have perhaps of happened had the army not intervened. In the chaos that happened, youth gangs looted shops, beat people and could have swept the state into anarchy.

To save vital resources and integrate people into accepting different faiths, I think it would make sense to encompass all legal religions under the Distributist government in a single church, instead of having separate churches for different faiths. By doing this, religion will be more diverse and therefore people will have more freedom to believe in whatever they choose to believe in, from Science to Spirituality to Paganism to Christianity. Cathedrals should be remodelled to encompass all religions except Islam in separate areas of the building. For instance, in a cathedral, in one (or two, depending on size) room it will be dedicated to teaching Orthodox Christianity, another would be Paganism, another Protestant Christianity, another Catholic Christianity, another should be the 'New Religion' etc. To accommodate the larger areas of religion churches and cathedrals will practice, many will have to be enlarged, depending on how many in the local area go the place of worship.

It is pointless and risky having a state supporting only one religion. People should be able to choose whatever faith they believe in, with the exception of Islam which poisons the minds of young people, the Islamic State dictating the absolute utmost faith in Islam at all times with the consequence of being executed. Evidence suggests half or more of the past wars in history, especially in Europe, have been fought over religion. In Medieval Russia for example, there were arguments between the Tsar or the Grand Prince and the

Orthodox Church's control of the Monasteries, which claimed vast amounts of land. Other examples would be the Crusades, in which the vast remainder of Pagans in Europe were brutally Christianised. Therefore, it is much wiser to support all people's faith they choose to believe in. War over religion is far from being extinct as well, the unstable Middle East is the prime example.

The recent campaigns against the Islamic State should speed up their offensive, the bombings will only make the terrorists want revenge and thousands of innocent people are dying at the hands of NATO bombers and ISIL executions. Not a day goes by now when some unlucky innocent person dies at the hands of the Islamic State. The Islamic State militants are evil and primitive people, believing that Islam is all powerful and everyone should have unquestioned faith in it, they relentlessly kill innocent people, record it and send it online where the victim's family members have to witness these primitive people's justification for killing the person and then the prompt beheading of the victim. The fact they decide to torture the victim and the victim's friends and family is disgusting and immoral. The way they justify these killings is primitive and simple-minded.

More recently, the Muslims have been blaming the Jews for their crimes, similar to how the Nazi's blamed everything from causing Germany to lose World War I, communism and the Great Depression. It is completely unjustifiable how these Muslims blame the Jews in order to get away with their petty terrorist attacks. The Muslims, despite being already so populated and vastly outnumbering the global Jewish population, are still against the tiny Jewish state of Israel's independence. The Jews in my opinion, deserve their own state, to protect them from Anti-Semitism aggressors such as the likes of the Nazi's and it is only fair they should rightly have their strip of land, especially if you compare Israel to the rest of the Middle East. It's disgusting how these people can terrorise Jews after the devastating Holocaust, which still affects some Jews today. Like the Nazi's, they seem to be pinning all their problems on the Jews to shift the blame away from the real aggressors which is no one but themselves. Their attacks on Jews are like spitting in the face of the devastated Jewish families who suffered from Hitler's Holocaust. Their recent attacks on the Jewish population are another reason out of many why the Muslim population should be removed from the UK.

For this reason it would make sense to keep the terrorist armies occupied and encourage the innocent Muslims to migrate from Islamic State territories. After many of the innocent people are out of the territory, it would make sense to nuke the terrorists, it would save thousands of Allied troops from being killed and all the Terrorists will die a quick death. The Terrorists deserve it, after all it is likely that if the Terrorists had nuclear weapons, they would no doubt attempt to use the, against Israel or some other NATO country, which could escalate into another World War which could have devastating consequences for the United Kingdom. Their brutal executions of innocent people in ISIL territories, in which they show no remorse whatsoever, make it seem like they wouldn't hesitate to launch an attack on the US or the UK if they had fully deployable nuclear weapons.

After the terrorists in the Middle East around the world have been dealt with, the state should make sure there are no Muslims at all in the UK, otherwise there would be a risk of potential uprising. After the UK and more nations are under Distributist power, then states with imperialist ambitions could seize parts of the Middle East for themselves in order to secure the stability of the Middle East under a great empire. The recent invention of online social media sites have made the brainwashing of young people much easier for the Islamic State and their private websites make it difficult to find out where they keep prisoners. I also suggest once the terrorists and Muslims are all expelled from the UK, it would be important to set up a missile defence system around the borders to ensure safety from potential terrorist attacks in the future, especially if terrorists develop or occupy nuclear or powerful chemical weapons.

The final verdict on this chapter is to simply come out of the EU and persuade the US to nuke the Islamic State territory after ensuring many non-terrorists have left the state and prisoners in Islamic State territories have been liberated. Also equally important thereafter is to ensure that all Muslims are expelled from the country, by force if necessary, to prevent an uprising and terrorist attacks in the future on UK soil. Ban Islam as a religion, anyone suspected of being a Muslim should be chucked off UK soil by force. Designated areas where these Muslims go aren't of much importance, as long as they are out of the UK and its borders. The risks of nuclear war are too great, and if the Muslim terrorists successfully win a civil war, a Islamic dictatorship will emerge, shooting anyone suspected of not being Muslim (evidence is of the Islamic State militants beheading non-Muslims.) and causing a general state of poverty, filth, chaos, social unrest and riddled with crime. Immigration itself should be limited to a maximum of 50,000 a year.

The Muslim population in Britain is rising rapidly, giving they breed like rats, its estimated that in 20 years' time there will be 6 million Muslims in Britain, that's 1 in 10. It's important to expel them from Britain before their population becomes too risky to deal with. Designated areas for terrorists could be to the Middle East or willing European states. Drop-off locations which are close to the French borders such as Ashford or Margate should be prioritised, where they will be punished by way of having to swim to the French shores. Otherwise, Islamists could be sent to the Middle East by way of air travel. Muslims who are non-terrorists could be sent to some of the UK's remaining oversea colonies, although it would be preferable for the, to be sent off elsewhere, somewhere where they can never again threaten UK stability, social order and freedom.

Chapter 2

Distributism, Collectivisation, Industrialisation and the weakness of currency

Modern society lives on one thing: money. Money makes everything in today's world; even countries rely on their GDP to have a rough idea on how powerful/strong their economy is. Money has been around for thousands of years, dating as far back as the Ancient Greeks. However, only in recent times has money begun to show its darker side. With the rise of Feudalism in Europe and more recently, Capitalism; states have begun to exploit how money is distributed in their countries. There are vast differences between how rich the general population of a country is, for instance you have the wealthy in Monaco and Switzerland and then there's the poor living in poverty in most parts of Africa. In countries in the European Union, there is a trend which has been going on for many years now. the richer get richer while the poor will get even poorer. I dare say that if it keeps on going like this, there won't be a middle class any more, just the very rich and the very poor. In the United States, there are more homeless people than there are vacant houses.

A country that relies on a currency-based economy is limited to how much resources the government can take and make things out of. Whilst this can be a good thing to an extent, in order to save resources by putting a price on them, it isn't necessary in modern society. Many resources can be recycled and reused over generations, becoming out-dated, recycled, and then reused in the improved next generation. Other things can be preserved for considerable amounts of time, which makes surplus production of materials not go to waste. Jobs in the near future will be very scarce, as A.I. improves people will become abundant, resulting in mass unemployment throughout the world which will inevitably cause mass hysteria. Like in the Industrial Revolution, before everyone had to make literally everything by themselves without machinery. The new technological breakthroughs will continue to eat away at the declining workforce; Human-like AI is inevitable at some point.

If cyborg technology becomes a mainstream reality in the future, which it probably will, giving how fast computer processing powers are accelerating; I would ban people from upgrading their brains to process things more quickly and ban people from utilising robotic parts altogether. In order to save the Human race from extinction, from evolving into robots, I feel that it would be necessary to do such a thing. Of course if this ever did happen, especially in states that have a currency, there would be a growing threat of civil war as the poor or Class 4 and 3 citizens won't be getting these upgrades, and they will be replaced by more intelligent cyborg people which inevitably will cause a mass civil war. Also the Class 1 and 2 citizens or the rich people who choose not to have the modifications, will probably eventually end up being replaced in many of their jobs too.

Robots, unlike Humans, don't need sleep, food or drink, therefore many industries will benefit from AI controlled cars in the future. Lorry drivers will become abundant, as will eventually shop keepers, when upright, walking AI androids become widespread. Nannies and servants will become unnecessary with the widespread arrival of the robots you see in so many Sci-Fi films that will someday, within the majority of many of our lifetimes, become reality. The trouble only starts there, if robots surpass Human intelligence and the robots begin to recognise they are being treated as slaves, there will be an unexpected uprising. Other risks include the hacking of computer systems, including all forms of AI which could then be used against humanity. Therefore it is imperative to at least restrict AI research for a time being, probably forever.

Also, we shouldn't become too dependent on machines, as in the event of hacking of all AI interfaces, we will be completely defenceless against the wrath of the machines we built. Therefore only basic industrial machines which don't have any way for AI to interact with it at all should be allowed, and the military should restrict the number of AI-controlled weapons, humanoid robots of destruction and vehicles and aircraft.

In order to stop the AI revolution from happening and reduce inequality, a state simply has to dissolve its currency and its economy as we now know it. People in the present time have been brought up around money, many being raised and nurtured until it's time for them to go out into the 'big wide world' where it's their destiny to find a job and earn money, to live. For some people, they can't imagine a world without money, they don't see how society would run, how it would work, partly because they've been brought up around money however if a person with a slightly broader, wider mind thinks about it, they will find that it doesn't have to be like this.

Of course most people need a purpose in life, a job plays a big part. People could still have jobs; society could run just as it is now without money, without the unfair wealth distribution between the rich and poor, without the greed of governments and rulers and every citizen getting enough food and drink to stay alive. This is possible, for instance if said state dissolves its currency and introduces the concept of wealth classes. Some might ask why have put a value on things when there is no currency, the answer is, everything needs some value, otherwise eventually everything will run out. For instance, if there was no value of food, people could just waste food and eventually there would be too many humans on the planet to feed. Same goes for valuable products, such as things used for construction. Also, I believe it is necessary to have some people more well off than others, for instance a person who works hard all his life deserves more than a person who does nothing for the world and expects other people to look after them.

Wealth classes are four classes whom every citizen of said state comes under. To show people what class they are before they acquire their items, a stainless steel rectangular card-shaped item with their class number, name, date of birth, sex and place of birth imprinted onto it. Stainless steel will be ideal as paper or plastic cards could get damaged easily.

Class 4 is the lowest class and includes immigrants who have been residents of the country for less than 3 years, regardless of occupation. Also under this class are the people who don't work at all. All classes collect food once a week to last them until the next, though for Class 4 people the amount is typically very minute and generally unhealthy fast-foods. All Classes will have bigger houses depending on how many people there are in the individual house. For instance a Class 4 citizen living on their own will probably just have one room and one bed. Electric is provided with a microwave included. Class 4 houses don't have the luxury of central heating or gas, low quantities of coal is used instead to heat their apartments. A single small window and curtains will be present in the apartment. Since only Class 4 citizens will be living in the same building together, there will be toilets, showers and a laundrette outside the building for Class 4 people. Most Class 4 people should be housed into skyscraper buildings, to utilise and save land area.

No more than 6 people can live together in any class, as no more than 4 children are permitted to citizens. Class 4 people will be restricted to using buses to make their way around. Class 4 people will have to have one of every area of clothing, and should be limited to what they can choose. Entertainment wise Class 4 people will be able to get second-hand cheap toys for children, an optional kids toy box as well. Adult entertainment should be restricted to three magazines/newspapers per week for each Class 4 person of their choice. Hospitals should be available to all Classes; however things like plastic surgery or breast implants will be available to Class 1 and 2 citizens only. Pencils and paper will be offered to each individual Class 4 citizens optionally. Perhaps the most valuable thing a Class 4 person (over 12) is offered is an old mobile phone with the Internet on it.

Class 3 citizens will include people who work 2 hours a day on average or 14 hours a week in total. If a person of this class doesn't do at least 14 hours a week like all the other people in the class, then it is legal for their employer to take one of their possessions off of them, to punish them. If a Class 3 citizen fails to work 14 hours a week repeatedly, then they are fired from their job and downgraded to Class 4. Said citizen has to have 2 years of their life under Class 4 before they are allowed to enter any Class 3 job. The jobs Class 3 citizens have can be any of the options offered by the state with the individuals ultimate choosing of one of the jobs presented to them by a State official will all require 14 hours work time weekly. Class 3 people's and those above this class (Class 2 & 1) also have the right to go to enter museums, amusement parks and go out to a restaurant of their choice three times a week. In the case of museums and theme parks, though, in Class 3 it should be restricted to no more than 4 hours in museums and no more than 4 hours in theme parks monthly.

New jobs will be available as supervisors or State Officials (SO), whom will be responsible for checking if people are doing the correct amount of hours for their respective class, and informing their superior if they aren't doing the right amount. They are also responsible for suspending citizens from their class for two years if they repeatedly underperform in their job or they aren't doing enough. State Officials class number comes under which ever class level they are monitoring as their profession.

Class 3 citizens should be allowed to watch a film at the cinema 10 times a year, a state official at the cinema will have to keep track of the number of times the individual has been to the cinema and restaurants by checking the electronic class number of the individual, which will have a security code for the state official to unlock, which will subsequently change yearly. After unlocking the security code, the electronic card number will detail the amount of times the individual has been to, at given dates. After ensuring the individual has not broken any laws under their class, they finally establish a record of the date and that they've gone to the cinema/restaurant.

Class 2 and 3 citizens will take up most of society in an idealistic country, to have a highly populated middle class and a therefore fairly distributed wealth to pedestrians. Unfortunately if this form of wealth would ever happen, it would be virtually impossible for a two adults of two different classes to share a house with one another as there would be no real way of determining which Class that particular household comes under and without a specific class number, there isn't a practical way of determining how large their house should be as they don't come under any class.

To be a Class 2 citizen, you would have to work at least 35 hours a week. All full time soldiers in the armed forces will also be a part of the Class 2 wealth class. Class 2 citizens get substantially larger houses than Class 3 citizens, quicker Internet speeds, a reasonably sized TV for each bedroom and a larger one in the living room. A gaming console is available for individual Class 2 citizens every 4 years, meaning they gain a console of their choice every four years, with 15 games, 24 DVDs/Blu-Rays and 15 books of their choosing per year. Class 2 citizens, then aren't short on entertainment. Class 2 citizens get other luxuries such as being entitled to going out for dinner 6 days a week of their choosing, more comfortable chairs and beds, a better car, 20 opportunities to visit the cinema per year, unlimited museum and theme park times and a better looking house than Class 3 citizens with the house being detached as well.

Class 1 citizens are reserved for people who lead a large business (all business itself though are owned by the state), movie stars, musicians, successful film directors, successful authors, famous and successful athletes, high-ranking government officials, high-ranking military commanders etc. Class I citizens, at least ones with families, get large mansion sized homes, fully-customised to their liking with a huge garden and are entitled to either go out for food anywhere every day or have highly sought after meals at home. They can optionally have their own maids and servants as well. Class 1 citizens are only available to people aged 21 years and over.

Class 1 citizens can retire when their 45, Class 2 can retire when their 65 and Class 3 when their 75. Citizens less than 18 years of age are entitled to their parents class number, however once they are 18, unless they are at College or University they are no longer entitled to their parents class number. If a citizen goes to College or University, they lose their parents class number once their 20 years old.

This form of government, Distributism, will reduce inequality among people, isolating people who refuse to work and the inferior-minded in Class 4. Under this political system, the state can still distribute the most materials available towards the higher classes, still having control over how much resources the national population takes despite the absence of currency through the use of the wealth class system. Education should be strictly focused on the students future career, and by the end of school the individual has choices which result from how well they did in exams, for example if a person performs poorly in Maths and does well in English, they will be encouraged to become a journalist, an author or a librarian. The individual, based on their exam results will ultimately decide which job out of the jobs on offer which is suitable for their expertise they would prefer to do.

By controlling to an extent what people pursue once they leave school, will noticeably improve levels of skill in all areas of the workforce, whilst individuals themselves would still have a high degree of freedom to choose which job they want to pursue based on the subjects they did the best at. By enforcing state control over aspects of a future job for a young person, it should make unemployment lower by making sure the individual gets to be employed in the job preferable to them. By making an overall better choice of freedom on jobs, making workers overall happier, will therefore also improve the level of effort by all workers overall.

People will thereby be happier in their jobs, they will have more of a purpose and work efforts will increase, increasing the overall position of the economy by the use of collectivisation that is collecting the nationalised resources not needed by people and the state using them for military and construction use. By having state control over young people's careers therefore will reduce inequality because the individual will only be able to pursue what is available to them, based on their educational results. It would stop inferior people from having high-ranking jobs or becoming rich, preventing people doing nothing at all from gaining loads of money. Instead there will be wealth classes, which will overall distribute a much fairer society. The intelligent will be rightly placed in Class 1 and 2, preventing the potential of an intelligent individual's failure in a job interview as opposed to a person of lesser skill and knowledge.

Getting rid of currency and replacing it with wealth classes plays a role in stopping starvation, as even under Class 4, a person gets reasonable amounts of food, and under wealth classes, by distributing food to all classes precisely, no food goes to waste either, which happens so often now in developed countries, especially the rich whom waste large amounts of their purchased food if they don't like it. When you look at the people who are obese in developed countries stuffing more than enough food in their mouths and then comparing it to many parts of Africa where people are too poor to purchase enough food to keep them healthy. So the 16.6% of the people living in the UK will go above the poverty line and most of them will get jobs. Also mothers won't be getting more benefits than needed under Distributism, thus women won't just have children for the sake of grabbing all the benefits anymore. One thing all classes should share though is the equality of rights, discrimination shouldn't be allowed at all. We are all humans and we all have feelings at the end of the day.

Discrimination/racism can severely reduce a workers output, can easily lead to depression and once a worker continually begins to underperform in their job, they will rightfully be removed from their respective class and be downgraded into a lower class in which they don't have to work as much. To remove a good, hard-working person from their rightful job because of the evil discrimination against them would be a huge shame for the person and the Distributist government itself. People deemed guilty of discrimination towards their fellow work mates should be removed from their post, and as further punishment, lashings on their back by the use of a whip used by their superior. This will inevitably stop discrimination in the labour force considerably, decisive action is needed to make sure that the work force is disciplined, well behaved and works to their maximum to ensure the equal Distribution of food and drink to all classes and making sure that the lowest class get adequate housing facilities.

As part of distributing the economy through the use of wealth classes, all business should be controlled by the state, all construction works should be done by the state. The central government in London must have complete control of the whole country, State officials enforcing order in different counties. Independent companies which are not controlled by the state, goes against Distributism and its ideology, to enforce everything is distributed perfectly among people. The state should utilise all its resources, first giving all people the amount of resources needed for their respective class, the equal Distribution of food being the top priority, and then using the remaining resources for the construction of business buildings, offices, flats, military usage etc. All resources and business, then, even if foreign, must be nationalised and taken under government control. Britain, or any other society in the world, will benefit in the short-term by being more productive in a year than perhaps five years under a state with currency. In the long run, the government can control the population and distribute resources best-suited to the country at the time.

Heavy use of Rapid Industrialisation will be needed to provide all classes with their products, who will depend on the self-sufficient industry to make their products promised to their individual class numbers under state law. Factories should only be present in large cities and colonies off mainland Britain in order save land mass needed for homes and offices, making Britain itself the dominant area by population. The country itself would survive by production of raw materials and farming alone, the large Arctic territories will help render the needs of the population of the mainland. Preservation of surplus produce will be an important factor in not wasting and getting the most of our raw materials, obsolete products such as outdated military weapons and broken items which retain some good condition to be used as upgrades later on. Recycling plastics and other recyclable items will also be compulsory to every citizen. The use of Distributism, state controlled Collective farms and an extremely large industrial sector will emerge a state not influenced by currency, with a much fairer society, distributed perfectly through state control of young people's careers and a happier workforce.

Chapter 3

Population and Environmentalism

The world is still growing in population at a fast rate, at 7.3 Billion, that's 300,000 more people than 2011 when world population reached 7 Billion. The cause of this is simply with the advent of new, evolving technology people are getting older, easily going past 80 in developed countries. World population has really only began to boom with the invention of industrialisation, population has more than quadrupled in 100 years alone, whereas before world population was increasing very slowly. In fact, from 0AD to medieval times, some believe the world population actually decreased slightly, which would make sense due to all the horrific plagues and outbreaks of disease that were powerless to stop in them days.

For instance in 1750, world population was estimated to be 791 million. It wasn't until 1802 when it reached 1 billion. The 19th Century was comparatively slow as well. Population was only 1.64 billion in 1900. However by 1950 it increased to 2.52 billion, and the 'baby boomer' generation drastically increased population levels to a staggering 6 billion by the end of the century. So it is really only in the past 60 years or following the Second World War, with the advances in medicine, and more successful births of babies that the population has really took off. From 1995 to 2000 world population increased by 6.98%, which in previous centuries took decades.

Also in many Asian countries such as India and Muslim countries, still often have families of 6 or more children even though India is hugely overpopulated already. In countries such as Mongolia, Russia, Canada and Australia population is comparatively scarce, if anything there should be more people in lesser populated countries rather than ones in densely populated countries due to the strengthened effects of pollution in densely populated areas. In the near future overpopulated countries, especially ones relying on trade and imports from other countries will starve. For this reason countries will go to war with each other over water, food and land, which could perhaps lead to another World War, only this time there will be much more devastating weapons involved.

Having more than three children will be illegal under all classes. I feel this is necessary in order to control the population. Taking this even further, I would restrict the number of immigrants coming to the country and in desperate circumstances, ban immigration altogether. However I wouldn't totally ban population growth, I would let the population grow to a reasonable 99 million at its maximum, counting all British colonies as well, as I will explain in the next chapter, I will increase the land mass of the state, therefore allowing the state to reach a maximum population of 99.9 million. If the population starts to go over this limit, then drastic measures should be taken. The complete ban of immigration, lowering maximum quantity of babies per woman and also perhaps forcefully removing lower Class 4 people in dire circumstances.

Coastal countries who are non-Distributist such as former Indochina, many major cities in the United States and small islands will suffer extensive flooding in the near future if they don't take the option of spending huge amounts of money on coastal barriers, to refugees such as of these crisis' should be rejected British citizenship if the national population starts to exceed 99 million. The immigrants who do come should be restricted to a maximum of 50,000 a year and will have to fully integrate into British way of culture, instead of speaking in their native language, for instance. Also I would restrict efficient synthetic organs and longevity medicine to Class 1 citizens only, to stop too many people from living longer and potentially becoming immortal which would result in a great population explosion.

All settlements should be standardised under a system which controls a settlement by way of its name. The national village population should be at 5,000, towns 50,000, 'standard' cities: 250,000, large cities 2 million and London 13 million. The city of London should be expanded slightly to accommodate the staggering population, and flats and offices with no historical value or beauty which are deemed too short should be demolished to make full use of London's land area. Once the population reaches 100 million, 17.4 million (20% excluding London) should be living in villages (4,480 villages), 29.57 million should live in towns (588), 26.1 million in standard cities (104) and 14 million in large cities (7). England should continue to take the bulk of the population at 50 million, with Scotland up to 22 million, Ireland 12 million and Wales 7 million. Colonies should be at 9 million, there usage mainly being their resources and lands to build factories and labour camps in order to retain Britain itself as the dominant area of the British Empire.

The reasons to restrict the population are obvious: there are simply not enough natural resources to sustain the Human population, especially if the population continues to grow like it is now. At a global population of 3 Billion, I would say or guess that the population is relatively controlled, however once the population becomes far beyond that number, we will eventually starve and our population will (theoretically) eventually die down after years of starvation. Of course we don't want future generations to go through a devastating war, Because of their ancestors failed system. Unfortunately it is bound to happen at some point if we don't do something serious about the growing population. We are already a pest, nothing more than an intelligent pest, rapidly draining the resources of the Earth at an increasingly faster rate, which will ultimately culminate in an apocalypse, possibly World War III.

Also people and other animals alike deserve their space. When the later state colonisation of uninhabited, unclaimed places takes place, there should be a national rewilding effort. By doing this, combined with punishing poachers severely, by punishment consisting of potential decades in prison, we could help save many species of animals from extinction. We are not God, so why do we always cull the population down whenever wildlife becomes involved in some stuck up rich person's backyard?

My guess is that us, Humans still haven't gotten over the fact that animals are now rare, and that we are now the pest, not them. For some reason, most Humans do not get it into their big skulls that animals are endangered, and that most Humans don't need any other animals apart from the Domesticated animals for food anymore. That is why it is completely unnecessary to hunt and poach animals for a living now, because all food is now commonly available in supermarkets. In fact more than enough food is available in the supermarkets at the moment, hence why the equal Distribution of food to all classes should be implemented by total state control over resources. There are also growing numbers of sadists out there thanks to the growing population whom kill animals for pure fun in a sadistic manner.

By having the equal Distribution of food as the state's top priority, it will prevent starvation to all people within the UK, while at the same time prevent food from being wasted by simply producing too much food for the population. Families will be given their choice of food, with the higher classes getting the same amount albeit with more choice, and will not dare waste what they get, as that will only be what they get that week. The government shouldn't have to keep on supplying benefits to those pathetic people who do nothing but eat and don't bother to help themselves. Some of the obese people that swarm the streets of the UK at present consume more food a day than a person in Africa does in a whole week. The quantity of food shouldn't be different to the rich and poor, most people have the right to eat just as much as anyone else, therefore the equal Distributist collectivisation of food and drink will prevent people from starving and others from eating more than what they need.

There is a growing trend that the higher the Human population is, the more animals in the wild seem to go extinct. The general animal extinction process has been sped up significantly during the previous century; an example would be the passenger pigeon, like a common pigeon in the 19th century, was then brought to extinction in the early 20th century, due to the disturbing of their nests and the selling of their eggs. Other examples include the Dodo, a flightless bird which was hunted to extinction within decades of Human arrival on the island it inhabited. The Moa and the Haast's Eagle in New Zealand too were bought to extinction, the Moa was hunted for its meat, it was the largest flightless bird and was bought to extinction because of it. The Moa's predator, the Haast's Eagle, in return was bought to extinction along with it due to its main source of food dying out.

Even animals with such high-culture such as the African Elephant and the Giant Panda, are estimated to be extinct by 2040. If this is true and happens, this generation will be the last to see these magnificent creatures. Perhaps the biggest reason for poaching in modern society is due to the valuable prices of ivory, such as the tusks and horns on Rhino's and Elephants. Fur is also expensive, along Reptilian skin. The poachers tend to sell them to countries such as China, who still holds the traditional belief of extreme values in animal parts for medicine. Japan is responsible for a lot of the over-fishing that occurs in the Pacific Ocean, even cutting off shark's fins to sell as shark fin soup and then chucking the shark into the sea bleeding to death and defenceless. The prices of animal products which give poachers the incentive to illegally poach animals is another important reason why currency should be completely banned. Zoos should be built in areas which are not used by people, Elephants and Rhino's should be escorted to the UK where they will hopefully breed, then perhaps the young could begin to venture out into the wild, when the climate is estimated to warm up thanks to emissions.

Class 1 and 2 people; at least, deserve some garden, not like how it is in urban cities now where they just cram all the flats in together like a ton of bricks in a line. The only people living in small flats under Distribution rule will be Class 4 citizens only. Also it's not fair on the wildlife when their habitat is increasingly destroyed and subsequently habited by Humans which is why we must restrict the population level to a sufficient amount and distribute people in UK soil more evenly, making villages larger and cities (with the exception of London) smaller. In some cities it is far too cramped full of people, cities like Birmingham, Sheffield, Cambridge etc. are far too busy. The industrial factories of large cities that need the production to sustain the population also takes too much of a toll on the Earth's atmosphere. In contrast, rural areas such as in many parts of Scotland, and Scottish islands and some parts of northern England need to be populated more, or distributed more evenly.

To help prevent a country, especially one overpopulated from starvation and thirst in the future it is necessary to utilise vertical farming, which are skyscraper-like buildings which have farms in them. By having super tall vertical farms, it would put land to better use, saving loads of land by destroying the old style farms and replacing them with wildlife reserves instead, for a national rewilding effort and it will add more culture to the state. By abolishing old traditional farms which are spread over a large area, it will make the necessary living space requirements for the higher classes, as well as national parks and military training grounds. Another advantage for Vertical farming is that it protects its produce from rainfall and pollution, rendering crops healthy and fertile.

A typical vertical farm, in order to best utilise land area, needs to have a target of being at least 1000ft tall, along with a bulky width and depth to store different rooms of crops in the farms. Most British colonies will house vertical farms, with villages having their own vertical farms labelled as theirs in a colony as part of self-sufficiency. 10 farms will be needed to supply a town and 50 for a standard city. To prevent animals from forests where farms used to be from running out onto roads, fences should be built along these particular roads to prevent all sorts of animals from running out.

Hydrogen, Hybrid and Electrical powered cars will be the future, with oil powered cars becoming rarer as it is running out fast. By having alternate powered vehicles, emissions will be cut down, decreasing the risks of further polluting the atmosphere. It is important to utilise Wind, Hydrogen, Solar, Fusion and other renewable electrical energy to full extent, in order to replace the harmful substances of coal, oil and nuclear power as replacements for rapid industrialisation which civilians will depend on for their own products under Distributist rule. In order to achieve self-sufficient electricity, all buildings, including homes, schools and offices should have solar panels on them to generate electric from the sun. Vast quantities of advanced windmills should also be placed near coastal areas, preferably in shallow waters near coastal areas. By doing this, hopefully, all UK houses will have enough electric to keep warm.

I would also think about constructing underground homes, utilising the land underneath the Earth, even if it's just for protection from nuclear fallout. For sure, I think an underground bunker, near every house would be highly appropriate in the advent of war. Actual conventional houses for citizens though, should be restricted to Class 4 people only due to the smell of rubbish dumps underground. Class 1 and 2 citizens should get underground shelters for protection against fallout. At least then, the most intelligent, successful people of the state will have a better chance of surviving than inferior people. Nonetheless, underground houses would conserve a lot of land, as would super-tall skyscrapers with apartments in them, Class 4 and 3 people will take the bulk of the population in these mega 200 metres plus tall skyscrapers, utilising land and air to full extent. In London, I vision under Distributist rule I would fill the Canary Wharf with dozens of kilometre tall skyscrapers, when construction gets slightly more advanced and we have the resources to do it. It would make the city of London look great and futuristic and it would add a lot of depth in terms of general historical interest in contrast to the older and smaller buildings.

In order to save island countries such as Britain from devastating floods in the future, mega-tall, thick water barriers should be built around all the borders of Britain and her colonies, with a door/gate in the barriers to let boats and ships go through, closing the door thereafter to protect Britain from the oceans rising sea levels. Due to climate change, global warming specifically, polar ice caps are melting and in turn forming water which raises sea levels. Every year the sea rises a few millimetres which is very scary when you consider how much it will be over a few hundred years. The coastal barriers should be at least 200 metres tall and surround all of the borders of Britain like the walls of a castle, the reason why they need to be this tall is in the event of a massive freak tidal wave which is sometimes reported to happen and destroy and flood settlements. Inside Britain itself, on land, rivers should also be taken with caution, I suggest 5ft barriers be built among potential rivers or lakes that are prone to flooding. The River Thames in London should be suppressed by some sort of barrier as well, ideally 10 feet should be enough.

The other thing to do would be to make the atmosphere clean by seeking alternatives to production. For instance, the UK doesn't want to end up like India, with rubbish everywhere and filled with diseases, nor do we want to end up like China, who's insistence on industrial factories have caused urban areas to become increasingly polluted, causing many civilians to wear masks to cover their noses and mouths, acid rain and dust clouds. People in both countries are in general disgusting, the poor in India being bought up in sheer poverty, scattering through rubbish bins to find food. The Chinese are bad in general terms, having a tendency to spit on the floor and never seem to wash their hands.

It is unlikely we will ever end up like India, as long as we strictly postpone the population to 99.9 million, by force if necessary. As long as the population remains like this, with the increased land area, and people generally being tidy and recycling, all horrendous forms of India shall be eradicated. Recycling should be made compulsory and people should get some of their property damaged in return for them not recycling properly. Recycling will help prevent the inevitable pile-up of all the plastics and materials humanity cannot simply destroy. The national population of villages should be kept at about 5,000, towns 50,000, cities 250,000, large cities 2 million and London 13 million. Ideally, in total 588 towns should be built (29.57 million), 3,480 villages (17.4 million), 104 standard cities (26.1 million) and 7 large cities (14 million). This brings the population to roughly 87.07 million people excluding London. The rest of the national population should be in London which would be nearly or dead-on 13 million inhabitants.

Another idea has occurred, if we could use the sun as a form of burning all waste, we won't be polluting the Earth's atmosphere and the waste will surely be permanent gone. The weakness of this idea is that we don't know how much or if it will affect the sun. Though I guess, the sun being as big as it is, will be able to sustain Earth's comparatively weak small materials. The big question is how to transport the waste there. When Space flight becomes widespread, we could just send giant unmanned rockets on route to the sun's direction, carrying vast amounts of waste to it. The Distributist nations will theoretically be able to explore more of space more quickly than the countries with a national currency, as the non-Distributist countries will have to save up, which will probably take longer than an eager Distributist nation's complete reliance on their available resources. We could also perhaps extract resources from the moon and other planets once a permanent British settlement there has been established.

As mentioned before, the Distributist system will also reduce wasted products; citizens will only get what they can definitely eat. This will in turn, reduce the number of food been buried underground or otherwise being burned. Paper in particular gets continually wasted, such as receipts and unwanted mail. Although most is recycled, it can't be helpful to the workers who produce the paper for nothing. Thus receipts and other less-important items should be extensively revised when they come under control of the government and used only when needed. So by utilising Environmentalism, restricting population, Distributing people in order to sustain the atmosphere and wildlife and using innovative methods to save and best utilise land mass, all in all under Distributist rule the UK will be a much greener and prosperous country.

Chapter 4

Isolationism, Militarism and Decisive government

A one-party state is essential for a decisive government. Coalition and democratic governments fail to get things done quickly; a lot of things that are suggested are never put into action because of lack of support from other parties. To ensure the development of Distributism, it is important to establish a one-party state, led by a decisive leader known as the Emperor. Otherwise, if the UK had a Distributist coalition government, politicians may disagree on the statistics on the best way to distribute resources. Some coalition members may not be true Distributist's, and have a certain lack of faith in the ideologies of the party. Democratic Capitalist politicians are practically useless anyway; often they don't have enough power to make the slightest difference to their country. The economy in Democratic Capitalist societies is effectively run by the wealthy, making politician's involvement rather useless given how politicians effectively race their rivals to appease civilians and coalition governments which are caused by democratic voting only prevent decisive leadership being made, and therefore no progress.

Right-wing and democratic political parties in particular, especially the conservatives, will never accept Distributism. I'm confident a political party which has faith in my ideology will eventually overcome the opposing parties by number of votes. However, once the Distributist government is in charge, there will be no need for other political parties. All the other parties' ideas will be inferior to the Distributist party and therefore not needed. Also since there would be some opposition to the Distributist government to start off with, such as those who are wealthy yet lazy, immigrants, Muslims and those who get more than enough benefits. It would be highly risky for a Distributist government to stay in power if there turns out to be a considerable amount of opposition, so eliminating other political parties would ensure this doesn't happen legally. After about 100 or even 50 years of Distributist rule, those who are bought up in a Distributist society will see the unrivalled superiority of the system which will eventually culminate in the complete stability of the regime. The monarchy should be allowed to continue, at least for historical reasons. However the monarchy's role in politics should be restricted, the monarchs ideas should still hold some considerable influence to the party. The Emperor himself, will be like a Medieval monarch himself, ruling with absolute power.

The Emperor of the Distributist state should have unquestioned power to make up any law he chooses and rule with absolute power. Of course, when the leader dies there is the problem of ensuring leadership to another particular person who would rule just as well. For this reason, it should be vital to retain the Emperor's life as long as possible; possibly making him immortal if the technology becomes available. By making him immortal, it would ensure decisive, pro-Distributist rulership for at least a few hundred years. When the leader eventually dies, leadership should be passed on to whoever the leader chooses in his will. The will should retain the original powers of the leader to the successor, and make it absolutely clear to who is the successor, to prevent unwanted civil war.

In this sense, the Distributist leaders policies will thrive for a very long time, and at least when he dies he will pass the absolute decisive rulership onto whoever is more in tune with Distributism and the other policies in this manifesto. The freedom of speech should still be allowed, though, how far it will go is limited. Nonetheless everyone should voice their own opinion anyway. All citizens won't be able to vote due to the leaders choice on his successor, however their influence will no doubt have an effect on the decisions of the leader of the Distributist government due to the obvious risks of uprising and therefore, another revolution only this time targeted on the Distributist's. The Distributist leader should, despite being an autocrat, should have political advisors due to the risk of over-working and stress. No more than 7 of the highest-ranking Distributist party members (excluding the leader) should be part of the National Council that is the members who discuss events and policies. National Council members should be allowed to be elected by the people, though of course actual power and the choosing of a successor will remain with the Distributist leader. National Council meetings should be held every month, with the Distributist leader attending and having the ultimate decisions.

As I said before, WW3 could still happen due to the ensuing chaos that will develop in the future, around 50 years or less from now. Countries will fight each other not so much for land, but for water and food. Civil War could also happen in many countries that brashly delve too deep down into Artificial Intelligence technology. More countries are developing nuclear weapons and more so will in the future, which heightens the threat of mass extinction due to WW3. Pollution perhaps, could get so bad in heavily industrialised countries such as China that babies could come out deformed and people could die from the pollution in major cities if it gets too bad. The effects of pollution will no doubt frustrate governments, whom will strive for untouched, natural, healthy land free from pollution in countries such as Madagascar, Papua New Guinea and many parts of Africa and Oceania. This could cause a major war as well. The Middle East at the moment is still unstable, very much like Europe was in 1914, over 100 years ago. It doesn't help that terrorist groups such as the Islamic State are rising and making a name for themselves and major countries in the area run by corrupt politicians. An example is the North Korean leader, Kim-Jong Un. It only takes a dictator of a country like him, with nukes at their disposal, to do something stupid to start a massive war.

In order to try and prevent breakout of war in any country, I believe the safest way is for the country to be isolated from other nations, not getting into any arguments with other states and not making any alliances either which in the end caused WW1 and many other devastating wars which could have perhaps been restricted to just two nations. WW1 or the Great War, for example could have been restricted to just Russia and Serbia against Austria-Hungary if Germany wasn't in an alliance with Austria-Hungary. It's the same thing with Russia. If the Russian Empire wasn't allies with Serbia or hadn't let down Serbia for not supporting them against Austria-Hungary over a dispute of territory, it could have just been Serbia's and Austria-Hungary's war. The alliance system had a big part in the cause of WW1. Therefore an isolationist policy is a must-have policy. The main thing though, when it boils down to it in 50 years or so, is to have the people of your country, adequately fed and hydrated while also having formidable military in the dire times ahead helps.

For that reason it is important to become self-sufficient, through the use of the before-mentioned vertical farms and Distributism in previous chapters. When non-Distributist states starve to death due to the forthcoming nuclear war, they will not want to trade with us anyway and therefore we will have to use the superiority of Distributism and quelling the population as a means of keeping the population nutritioned. Being Self-Sufficient will also make war completely avoidable, the United States for example, had an isolationist policy in the First World War but still joined the war in 1917 as the war was affecting her trade with Europe. By restricting trade with other countries and making self-sufficiency as efficient as possible through Distributism, Vertical farms and living space, the UK under Distributist rule and other states who become Distributist will prevail against the inferior Capitalist, economy-reliant states. To improve self-sufficiency to the maximum, everything that is recyclable should be recycled. Especially in the case of demolished buildings and old equipment, much of their materials could be reused to build more modern and bigger buildings and equipment.

For sure, having a formidable military right now, especially in 50 years' time when global warming begins to render crops infertile and overpopulation becomes a major crisis, is vital for any country. I would make an exception of the A.I. laws for the military, allowing active soldiers to have bionic implants to enhance their strength and stamina when the technology becomes available. I would also make the military more of a force due to NASA's search for extra-terrestrial life. If NASA ever do find advanced alien life like our own, I think it is vital to be prepared for hostility, especially if they are even more intelligent than Humans. Once we start exploring a lot of the galaxy, I think we should consider attaining an advanced form of space warfare, as a united country, a united planet, in the event that we would be at least somewhat prepared if a hostile alien civilization invaded Earth. Once the Human race begins to colonise different planets that will be the time when countries will need to make some form of global alliance, in preparation for what could be out there in the massive universe.

So I would enforce militarism as a key part of policy to defend from foreign countries, who will no doubt eventually succumb to overpopulation, famine and full-scale war. That is why it is vital to have a missile defence system against nuclear powers, though it is unlikely they will use nukes as it will pollute Britain and then they wouldn't be able to efficiently drain the state of its resources as the resources will be contaminated with radiation.

Nonetheless, the military would still be needed to make living space in the future, in case we run out of land to build vertical farms to sustain the population. For this reason I suggest the colonisation of Antarctica and Greenland in the future. Both are huge land masses and both are expected to become warmer, therefore more habitable and fertile for crops in the future. I would use the huge space of Antarctica and Greenland for prime usage of vertical farming, cargo ships will transport the goods from the Arctic and Greenland to Britain, where all classes will get the proportionate number of food. I would also use the two places, though to a lesser extent, as industrial factories, where resources will be transported to Britain and construction of buildings on the mainland can take place. The Distributist un-reliance of currency will enable the restored British Empire to take full advantage of her resources. It is important to get these two as soon as possible, especially Greenland, before a government makes them sovereign countries, or colonised by a foreign Capitalist country. Greenland should be inhabited as soon as it is bought under British rule at 9 million, while Antarctica should remain uninhabited in an effort to retain the continents wildlife.

Emphasis should be made on the military, as it would provide more jobs for all classes; all classes should have the option to join the military once they leave school. This should result in a huge army; at least 1 million troops should be stationed in the Arctic to protect agriculture and production against foreign invaders. Ideally, once the population reaches its limit of 100 million, there should be at least 1.5 million active troops. I would reintroduce the draft, boosting the number of trained, equipped reserve soldiers to ideally 2.5 million in the process. Like in Antarctica, at least 1 million troops should be stationed in Greenland, with about 100,000 stationed in all other oversea territories. The remaining will be defending mainland Britain and Northern Ireland.

Thus, the military with 1.5 million active soldiers (roughly 3% of the male population) out of 100 million citizens, will take up a considerable bulk of the workforce in regards to men. Women, due to their lesser physique, should be restricted to communications and nurse roles, I expect no more than 150,000 women to be in the Armed Forces. The restoration of an Empire that is limited in population will enable the restored British Empire to become truly self-sufficient, though the use of the vast resources in Greenland and Antarctica and the State-controlled Distribution of the resources to each wealth class.

Out of the 1.5 million active soldiers, 800,000 of them should be in the army, 380,000 in the Air Force and 320,000 in the Navy. I suggest the development of massive, AI controlled robots in the army. At least 40,000 should be in service. These giant, humanoid robots should be used for offensive operations only, supporting and protecting the infantry as they too seize territory. The Army should be supported in offensive operations by advanced attack helicopters, at least 20,000 helicopters should be in operation by 2060. There should be even more fighter aircraft by this period, 25,000, and by this time they should have advanced considerably. Future aircraft need to have hypersonic speed, space like altitudes, unrivalled stealth gadgets, missiles covering the front, sides, top, and bottom and back of the aircraft, combined with an opening under the pilot's seat, which triggers a parachute in the event of engine failure.

Active army soldiers should be expected to exercise and train daily, at least a half a mile jog six days a week, 5 sets of 80 crunches four days a week, an hour of stretching 5 days a week, 5 sets of 40 press ups four days a week, a 3 mile walk carrying 30kg on their back 3 days a week and a boxing match twice a week. Active soldiers should also be fed healthy foods with lots of protein.

Reserve soldiers are expected to exercise less frequently, 4 sets of 60 crunches three days a week, 4 sets of 30 press ups three days a week, 20 minutes of stretching 3 days a week and a 2 mile walk carrying 25kg on their backs 3 days a week.
Ideally, the Navy should have 7 aircraft carriers, 50 submarines, 120 patrol boats, 20 Frigates, and 18 Destroyers. Meanwhile more effective, lightweight body armour should be developed for infantrymen and laser guns should be deployed in the Army and by warships. I also suggest the development of flamethrowers with longer ranges, to be developed in guns whilst retaining bullets, so soldiers can shoot and also burn their enemies from long distances. Long-range flamethrowers should also be deployed by Fighter aircraft as well. Force fields would make a major contribution to the defence of the borders, and it would give the military plenty of warning beforehand when opposition approaches. Force fields, should they ever come into use, should be incorporated around major buildings and landmarks in major cities, to prevent their destruction. As for force fields for use in other purposes, if scientists ever discover how to manipulate gravity, I suggest 'floating' force fields to be made in high altitudes above Britain, to give warning against incoming aerial attacks and the time to react. Also by manipulating gravity, land mass can be taken to full effect further through the colonisation of the skies.

Airships, or 'Goliath aircraft' should be implemented in the armed forces, a ship with the capabilities of being deployed as a formidable and large battleship as well as a formidable 'airship' would result in a Goliath aircraft, at 500ft long and 220ft in height, armed with extensive Missiles, Machine Guns, Laser Guns, Artillery and flamethrowers encompassed within all available areas for weapons under board the large airship (similar to an old Renaissance warship), with advanced electronic radars and highly accurate missile aiming systems will inevitably spark fear into enemy forces, providing a morale boost. The airships should hopefully achieve naval and air superiority in battle, adapting to various circumstances in battle, such as those of strategic importance or of avoiding death. The extensive armour on airships would ensure the airships tolerance of numerous attacks, and therefore achieve more destruction of enemy forces whilst surviving longer. When deployed as a naval vessel, the Goliath aircraft will resemble a heavily armed and armoured destroyer with aircraft wings which would fold up vertically onto the deck of the ship and should be at the front line of the Navy when at sea.

Multiple extremely large and powerful engines would be needed to propel the vessel to a high speed (100+mph) before the take-off is aided by the mechanised movement of the vertical wings to a horizontal position like in fighter jets, as well as the mechanised movement of the rear wing, which is propelled upwards from a flat position on the navy vessel resembling a downward tail, into a vertical, aerodynamically streamlined way similar to modern fighter jets. To guarantee a quick take-off, once the entire bottom half of the airship has submerged from the sea, a spacecraft propulsion launch should then begin on the basis of an electric ion thruster propulsion system. Once the airship is airborne, then the thrusters should be turned off due to the immense power, unless the pilot wants to reach a high altitude. Otherwise the engines and the aerodynamically effects of the airship should be able to maintain the current altitude like an airborne hovercraft. As a potential upgrade to a 'Goliath airship' giant helicopter turbines could be implemented in some to help achieve take-offs and higher altitudes more efficiently.

As for space warfare, once the Distributist government is in power, we should co-operate with NASA and the Americans to build fleets of spaceships, with hypersonic missiles attached at all sides to defend Earth from potential extra-terrestrial invasion. When laser gun technology becomes more powerful, then these spaceships should perhaps have these modifications done. Formidable spacecraft would be of strategic and vital importance especially if we find an advanced life form. Smaller space shuttles piloted by just one person should also be developed and once space warfare technology is underway, a British Space Force (BSF) should be established.

Given how much we know about the universe now, the fact there is a beyond-imaginative number of stars in the universe; it is extremely likely that there is an advanced race somewhere, like ours. In fact it is nearly impossible for there not to be given how huge the universe is, and how it continues to expand. With our aerial communications expanding rapidly, and the first Human trip to Mars to take place in the 2030s, we should begin to take a more cautious approach towards the universe itself.

That brings me again to my other reason for Self-Sufficiency and therefore, colonial expansions or building the vertical farms. If an alien invasion, or even a nuclear war does arise and most of the other nations are wiped out, we will be left to fend for ourselves. Therefore we mustn't rely too heavily on trade and interaction with the non-Distributist world.

After the first few years of Distributist rule, we should focus on spreading Distributism towards the rest of Western Europe, or come to talks with Russia about Distributism, them being used to the similar Communist ideology. I have a feeling we may get on well with some former Communist politicians or left-wing politicians in general. We will also probably get on well with Fascist states, and Imperialist states. We can show the foreign countries how great Distributism is, how it is going to turn the UK into a more equal, fairer and advanced nation, spread the word around that currency has had its time, wealth classes are superior. I am confident we will gain support from the working class and the poor no doubt. In many countries of Africa, we can spread Distributism easily and rapidly through here, as Distributism can promise all the African peoples are fed adequately and given shelter, regardless of class.

Once other Distributist governments are established, we will begin to co-operate with them to bring them to power and then we will begin to primarily trade with them and perhaps some major Capitalist countries such as the United States, Japan, Germany and China, providing it doesn't escalate into something like the Cold War. The Distributist expansion is similar to Leon Trotsky's idea of 'permanent revolution'. Once the Arctic colonies and other colonies that are vital to Britain's self-suffiency are annexed, a new and improved global peacekeeping force should be established, replacing the UN. The new peacekeeping organisation should be called the 'Alliance', and have a permanent defence force.

So it is henceforth vital to eliminate all other political parties once a Distributist government is in power, from there a young leader who is pro-Distributist will take absolute control and rule, for at least a few hundred years, in the process producing a much fairer and advanced society, isolate the state from the non-Distributist countries, colonise Greenland and Antarctica to save living space and build vertical farms and factories there and make significant progress with military technology and development.

Chapter 5

Laws and Order

Under Distributist rule, criminals will be sent to prison camps and receive a number of lashings from a whip depending on their crime or alternatively sleep deprivation, days of starvation and solitary confinement. In the workforce, when people are guilty of illegally discriminating against a fellow work mate, they should be removed from their position, if they repeatedly do it, lashings should be implemented and the amount should depend on the severity of the discrimination. 2 state officials (or 4-6, depending on the size of the building) will co-operate together to monitor all aspects of a particular work building, and will have to carry out their lashings as part of the punishment system for crimes. People who attempt to resist punishment and aggressors who attack state officials should be immediately sent to a prison camp, where they will be forced to do labour work for a few months, depending on how severe their rejection of the lashing punishment was. Captured terrorists should be sentenced to death by way of a clean beheading from the finest executioner and their corpses should be left out in the open for wildlife to eat.

If a Class 1 person is guilty of abusing their employees, they will receive a week in solitary confinement and fed poorly over the course of the week for going against the Anti-Discrimination policy, and thereby being disloyal to the regime. If a person is guilty of draining resources and selling them in a foreign country, they will be exiled to one of the oversea prison camps and receives 50 lashings over the course of 7 days for going against Britain by selling it to a foreign country. Punishments should be reduced to 25 lashes if the foreign country happens to be Distributist itself though. If a person is guilty of plotting to overthrow the government, they should be sent to an oversea prison camp and receive 40 lashes over a week for attempting to replace or overthrow the superior Distributist government

If people of a Class fail to do the necessary weekly amount of hours their class states (14 hours for Class 3, 35 hours for Class 2.), then they are at first, deprived of one of their valuable possessions for at least a week, their valuable possession eventually returns back to them providing they fulfil further work hours and work hard. If they fail to accomplish the necessary weekly amount of hours twice a month, then the individual receives 5 lashes from a state official and another possession of theirs took away. They will also be asked if they want to quit their job and seek another job within their class range. If a worker fails to fulfil weekly working hours four times in 2 months, then they will be removed from their Class number and de-ranked to the next lowest one for a minimum of 2 years and 2 weeks in solitary confinement.

To keep track of workers working times, a watch with the workers name on will set off as soon as the worker arrives and begins working, and then should be halted if the worker takes a break and then restarted again at the time which it was stopped after the worker returns and begins working again. To prevent complications for the State officials, workers should always go to the toilet once at a time and lunch breaks should all be at a designated time for all workers. This method of keeping a record of time on all workers should continue from Monday to Sunday, where all the watches will finally be stopped and restarted for the next week.

A similar punishment scheme applies to those who fulfil the necessary weekly working hours but fail to work as hard, or fail to put enough effort into their working hours. With industrial workers, this can easily be done by setting a task to a particular individual worker of a goal they have to reach within their weekly working hours. Slightly higher working efforts should be required in Class 2 jobs, therefore a Class 2 industrial worker must work slightly harder than a Class 3 worker does in fewer hours.

2 State officials (or 4 in larger buildings) will therefore closely monitor all buildings which houses workers working on their individual tasks, and at the end of the working week each worker will present to one of the State officials their work they have done, all individual workers times should then be checked using their individual watches which will record all the time the individual worker has done all week. After checking the amount of time the worker has done, the State officials should compare the amount of necessary time needed weekly (for instance 14 hours for Class 3) and then ensure that the worker has produced the minimum amount of work needed for the 14 hours. If the worker fails to produce enough work effort, then they receive 5 lashes from the State Official for 'unfair work effort distribution'. If a worker fails to produce the minimum work effort twice in a row, they receive 20 lashes and be asked if they would like to leave their current position. To prevent potential hostility from the workers, they should be clearly told and informed about their individual weekly minimum task, so in that way they cannot simply say they didn't know they had to do a certain amount of work. Workers should be told about their daily output every day, and be reminded of how much more they need to get done for the minimum weekly quantity allowance.

Weekly minimum output targets should be very achievable, but at the same time they need to be a little bit of a challenge to workers to provide enough quantity. It is pointless in having huge minimum requirements as the quality isn't good enough, and the workers time consuming jobs would be useless. Workers who fail to achieve a good enough quality of produce should be ordered to redo it until it is acceptable. If a worker does it twice in a row, lashing punishments should be enforced.

Meanwhile in Labour/Prison camps, prisoners should be fed minimalist food and drink, inmates aloud no more than 850 millimetres of water every 24 hours and food no more than 15 ounces per 24 hours. Food, as punishment for their crimes, should consist of their choice of drippings, a chicken head, duck feet, raw brains or balut. Anyone who refuses to eat the food will simply have to starve. Prisoners will also have to work well into the night, women and those under 16 waking up at 9:00 while adult males are woken at 6:00. All prisoners should have a 2 hour break from 13:00 to 15:00 and another for dinner from 18:00 to 19:00. All prisoners should be finally permitted to get some rest at dead-on midnight. Most prison camps should be built in Britain's oversea territories, so that Britain can utilise its supreme resources to full effect. Apart from a major prison camp being built near London, to show as an example to the people of the capital city what prison camps will be like if they do someone wrong, all other prison camps should be built in Antarctica, Britain's remaining oversea colonies and rural parts of Greenland.

Because punishments shall be harsh and disciplined under Distributist rule, I expect no more than 850,000 people, once the population reaches 99 million, should be kept in these camps, which means that overall a maximum of 85-90 prison camps should be built. Males and Females should be separated, and young offenders under the age of 16 should be kept with adult females and other young people under that age, to prevent unfair dominance of older male inmates to the younger, vulnerable ones.

As part of minimising the necessary resources to build the camps and as a means of punishment for prisoners, prison camps should all individually hold 10,000 prisoners, kept together in large cells in groups of 10. Therefore, 1000 large cell rooms will have to be built into a structure which utilises land space by being tall. All prison camps, with all-encompassing the same amount of prisoners, therefore, should all be the same structure. All prison camp buildings, to save land mass for the development of valuable vertical farms and factories, should have a hallway which separates the females and the people under 16 from the males, the hallway having the width of two prison cells put together (approximately 20ft wide and 40ft long) all prison cells should be square in shape and 7ft high from floor to ceiling. By having approximately 4x4 prisoners on one side and another 4x4 prison cells on the opposite side of the hallway, each floor would give 16 prison cells in total. To achieve the task of 1,000 prison cells, 63 floors would have to be built, each floor being 7ft tall, 60ft wide and 40ft long. The total height of the building therefore should be 441ft tall. Floor 63, with only 8 cells needed, will retain the height but with 4 instead of 8 at each opposite side of the hallway.

The London prison camp should be larger, 700ft. In order to intimidate Londoners as an example of what happens to some criminals, the London prison camp should be built specially out of stone, have no heating system or lights whatsoever and should resemble a 700ft tall medieval building. The terrorists and murderers who are executed by way of Capital Punishment shall have their bodies displayed inside the camp, as a constant reminder to prisoners of what happens to terrorists. In other camps though, their remains should be left out in the open to feed hungry birds. Once all the flesh has gone, then their corpses should be burned or buried. In the London prison camp, a large area should be designated as the prisoner's work place, where they will be put to work with building products from firearms to vehicles to toys. The materials they need for building will be exported from factories in

Greenland and Antarctica. In buildings which accommodate work such as factories and offices, a large room depending on the size of the building should be compulsory to house a place for solitary confinement, sleep deprivation and starvation.

As for laws, I believe the disgusting habit of smoking should be banned in public completely, as smoking is merely a drug people take to 'blend in' with their mates. It has no positive effects whatsoever, just negative bad health effects. By banning smoking completely, eventually within a month, all former smokers will eventually denounce their former smoking way of life and they will notice how bad it was for them and other people, and that it was the addiction that attached them to it. All tobacco should be banned, anyone suspected of growing tobacco should be exiled to prison camps in one of the British oversea territories by the police and receive 10 lashings immediately. I would also make it compulsory to redo your driving test at the age of 70, as I believe older people cause just as much accidents as the young inexperienced drivers on the road, perhaps even more.

To help eradicate slow drivers, minimum speed limits should be developed, 65mph on motorways, with a maximum of 100mph, a minimum speed limit of 15mph in villages and 35mph max. On country lanes, 80mph maximum and 50mph minimum. An exception should be made to those who break down and traffic lights. Slow drivers tend to cause accidents due to faster drivers wanting to overtake, some overtaking in dangerous positions and resulting in an accident. People who go slower (providing their car hasn't broken down) or faster than the speed limits will be pulled over, the police will check the drivers history and see if he has been pulled over anytime in the past 3 months. If they have, they are suspended from driving for 2 weeks. To make sure people don't ignore the suspension, their vehicles should be electronically tagged as an indicator to police vehicles that they shouldn't be on the road. After the suspension time expires, the driver can resume driving again like normal. If someone is guilty of causing an accident, they should be suspended from driving for 6 months.

To help the police catch prosecutors in order to pull them over, or criminals who have stolen resources, fast cars should be applied to all police officers. I suggest a fast four-door saloon police car which does 155mph and 0-100mph in less than 15 seconds as an adequate car for an individual police officer. The death penalty should be reintroduced, though only to mass terrorist attacks. Islamic terrorists in particular who happen to illegally be in Britain should be tortured before they are executed and should die a painful death, depending on how many people they killed and how much damage they caused. People who are caught littering by the police or on camera's will immediately get 1 lashing from the police and ordered to retrieve their rubbish and dispose of it properly. People who have been caught littering more than 3 times a month should be sent to the nearest prison camp, where they will immediately be forced to do back-breaking labour and be poorly fed. They will continue to be poorly fed and continually produce resources for the state for a week.

I would also make criminals such as murderers, in the fate of their victim's relatives or partner. I strongly think that if someone kills someone else, the victim's closest relatives or partner should get to decide the killer's fate, whether it's for them to be slaughtered or tortured using their own method and then serving life imprisonment or just being locked up for a certain amount of years. This way it will stop people from enacting vengeance on the murderer once they are set free from prison, allowing people to get their proper sense of justice from the murderer. This rule should apply to murderers only. If the victim is under 18 years of age, the victim's parents should have the ultimate say on the killer's fate. Otherwise, if the victim was over 18 and their parents are both dead, then their children, providing their 20 and over, should have the ultimate say. If they haven't got children, or the children are under 20, then the victim's partner should have the ultimate say. If the victim doesn't have a partner, children 20 years old or over or any parents, then the court itself should decide. If the victim's family decides to execute the murderer, options available should include hanging, beheading, burning, shot, the wheel, electrocution, poisoning, beaten to death, extensive torture/mutilation or a combination of these. The victim's relative or partner can also choose whether they themselves want to carry out the execution.

The Police force should patrol the streets like they did in the old days, and more people should be employed as police officers (whom entry level is Class 3). Ideally there should be 1 in every 120 people in a settlement patrolling the area. For instance, a village with 5,000 inhabitants will have 41 police officers, all split up into groups of 8 (with 9 at the most important area) patrolling five different areas of that settlement. The Police should be permitted to carry swords or small firearms to enforce order, whilst citizen ownership of a firearm should remain illegal, unless they have been or are in the armed forces.

Police patrols in urban areas should be doubled or even tripled in terms of quantity by percentage, due to the increased risks of crime in urban areas. For instance, for a large city of 2 million inhabitants, 1 in 60 should be patrolling the area. Important areas in cities where police groups are needed would be near places of importance, such as buildings where people go to work, shops, restaurants, landmarks, factories, farms, major housing estates, and educational buildings, places of worship and research labs. Sites which hold vital raw materials should also be guarded by the police, or by military bases, which I suggest be built near mining grounds and wildlife parks so the military can practice protecting the states resources and livestock from poachers.

Distributism, being a non-currency system and therefore not influenced by the value of currency, must rely on the states resources, helped with trade with other Distributist states, the careful, wise Distributism of the states estimated resources to feed and provide shelter for all different classes of the population, which will be number one priority. All punishments then are not at all handed out by fines, as there is no currency. To recognise all buildings as legally being government controlled and having faith in Distributism, all buildings should have the nation's flag somewhere on the exterior of the building as a compulsory accessory to the building. Police cars as well, should have the flag on the doors of their cars and sirens to differentiate them from normal civilian cars.

If State officials are found guilty of not carrying out their punishments to workers or of making a mistake in the timing system, then the police will arrest them and send them to a labour camp for a week. If they do it more than 4 times a year, then they are removed from their position. State officials, being the most dominant figure and the ones in charge of work buildings, are only answerable to fellow State officials, therefore only other State officials can rightfully accuse another of the crime. The same thing should happen with disloyal police officers. I expect not many, however will become disloyal to the Distributist government as long as the government maintains control of the educational system and therefore can dictate whom individuals get to be government officials, choosing the educationally able and those who have evidence that suggests they support Distributism. Soldiers in the armed forces should also swear an oath of allegiance to the Emperor and the monarch, the one's suspected of being the most faithful to the Distributist regime shall be promoted quicker.

Anyone suspected of abusing or mistreating animals should be sent to a labour camp for four weeks. If the individual happens to kill the animal in the process, then the punishment should be increased to fifteen weeks in the prison/labour camps, and receive 10 lashes immediately. The disgusting people who are found guilty of killing an animal and then attempting to sell it in foreign countries (as it would of course be impossible to sell it in Britain due to the superior Distributist wealth class system) or trading the animals remains (such as fur, teeth, skeleton etc.) should receive 30 lashes over a 72 hour period, a month of sleep deprivation and 6 months of imprisonment in a labour camp. Dead animal's remains must be buried or disposed of properly by their owners if domesticated for obvious reasons. The manipulation of an animal's corpse must be approved by the government itself, where the government should decide whether to simply ignore the request and order the burial, or instead choose to preserve the corpse and put it on display in a museum (if the animal is rare or a new species).

Sexual problems such as rape should be taken less seriously by the police, as many women tend to accuse men of rape in the most relaxed circumstances. For this reason, unless the woman shows clear evidence that she has been attacked and forcefully raped without the usage of a condom, only then it should be regarded as a crime. Being deprived of sex can lead to severe depression in males, as well as intense jealousy towards men who are successful with women. In order to prevent intense sexual urges by men onto vulnerable women, controlled sex should be allowed between strangers in the form of free prostitution, where neither person has to give something in return for having sex. Single women should be encouraged to take part in sex parties with desperate men and adolescent teens, where over time they will bond and manifest a proper relationship. In this way, society itself will be much happier (for at least, the men) from being much more open and willing to engage in sexual activities with strangers.

The flag, ideally under Distributist rule, should have a black circle in the middle of the flag, which represents militarism and permanent Distributist revolution. To the left and right of the circle should be green and red, split in half and separated by the black circle. The green represents environmentalism, nature and primitivism (to an extent in some areas, which is necessary to hold on to because of the robotic revolution.) while the red represents state control of everything, the fair distribution of wealth between classes and the different classes all united and working together in the best interests of the state everlong. All these colours, combined, represent the flag of Distributism.

So by enforcing these rather strict laws, workers will not dare to oppose the regime and all workers within the same class will have to work at the same rate and effort, or be punished strictly. This will eliminate class hatred, as everyone in the same class will be working at an even rate while those in higher classes will rightfully be rewarded more due to their longer and harder working hours as well as their profoundly better education results which the state itself dictates what class they shall live. State officials and police officers as well, will likely all be loyal Distributist's due to the consequences of disloyalty and the states control over who exactly should be an official. The result is Britain will have the most superior form of government and it will remain that way.

Chapter 6

Ideologies comparison and the weaknesses of Communism and Capitalism

Capitalism and Communism: two ideologies that was the cause of the Cold War and nearly caused total nuclear war or mutually assured destruction (MAD). Both are completely opposite, which explains why the Americans hated the Soviets obsession with Communism. Both ideologies have their strengths and weaknesses, Capitalism because Capitalist nations are usually corrupt because of individual's ownership of large business and the governments control over the economy which makes the politicians richer. Communism, too is bad as I believe while Capitalism tends to have too much of a gap between the rich and the poor, Communism takes away the sense of superiority of superior-minded individuals over less intelligent individuals, therefore taking ones purpose to 'work hard and you will be rewarded' down the toilet.

Nations under Capitalist rule tend to be corrupt, extremely nationalistic and imperialist countries, the old European colonial powers used their colonies as a means of extracting the resources from them and caring little for the conquered people, feeding them poorly, suppressing uprisings with brutal force and making them live in poverty, whilst extracting the resources from the colonies and bringing them back to the mainland. In fairness, though, these colonies the Imperialist powers used, eventually gained independence and many didn't really fare well off from being separated from the European empire's. Whilst under Distributist rule, Antarctica and Greenland will be annexed and colonised, there is a little number of people on these large masses of lands, so at least under Distributist rule, there won't be many people to treat differently anyway. British citizens who decide to immigrate to the conquered regions should be treated just like the wealth class system of the Central London government of the British Empire as a whole.

Examples include many countries in the Far East and Africa, the old colonial attitude seems to have gotten worse since the departure of their European masters in many of these countries and the gap between the rich and the poor is higher than ever. Overpopulation and the huge faith in backward religion remains an issue in many Far Eastern societies, with the fertility rate increasingly rising and the likes of India, Pakistan and Bangladesh seeming to never take a break from producing babies. Many of these societies have never advanced much further than the medieval era, many relying on western influence to help advance their respective economies. They fail to realise growing overpopulation, and the reasons behind the cause of overpopulation which is because more medicine is resulting in people living longer and more fertility rates. They also fail to realise the impact their vast overpopulated shambles of garbage are doing to the fragile ecosystem, many people not looking beyond chucking their increasing amounts of rubbish on the floor.

Different Empires had different levels of extremism to their colonies, the Japanese during WWII were probably the worst, brutally killing many of the conquered people and notably buried the Chinese alive in areas they occupied. They fed them hardly anything, and their method for treating the old colonial powers possessions in the Far East was comparable to Hitler's concentration camps and worse than Stalin's gulag prison camps. Nazi Germany, was strict and disciplined, and for that it was successful in enforcing total Nazi indoctrination of the German people. The Nazi's were also considerably advanced for their time, and had the right idea for Lebensraum (living space), Hitler had in which he planned to increase German land to save living space of the Aryan German people. However the regimes ethnic views and their wishes for a Slav slave race were not right and unethical.

In the Cold War, the United States recklessly defended corrupt nationalist regimes of the likes of South Korea and South Vietnam, because they were scared of 'losing' them to communism. In Vietnam, American search and destroy missions usually resulted in hundreds of innocent Vietnamese people being shot, the Americans lazily finding it easier to shoot everything that moves rather blindly. In the Cuban Missile Crisis, the ExComm 'hawks' hated communism so much, they wanted to risk nuclear war by launching the bombing of all Cuban missile sites in Cuba. The US Air Force general Curtis LeMay pressed Kennedy to launch the air-strike, had Kennedy approved this, there would of been nuclear war, as the Soviets actually had at least 20 nuclear warheads in Cuba already at the time. The Capitalist hooligans tend to act recklessly in times of what is perceived as a threat, they do not care of the consequences of nuclear fallout, and instead they see anything that is a threat to their wealth as the top priority.

Ignorant, wealthy Capitalist peoples were also partly responsible for Hitler's rise to power, as the wealthy landowners and business owners saw Nazism as a saviour of their precious wealth from Communism, which would take their wealth away. Had a similar scenario happened, with Distributism replacing Communism, the rightfully wealthy who actually deserve some of their wealth, would of therefore been less imposing on Distributism as opposed to Communism, as under Distributism, they are at least guaranteed some wealth, and if they are rightfully intelligent, superiority over some.

Capitalist nations, by having private business legal, make inequality far greater than what it would be under Distributist rule, as many business owners greedily seize too much money for themselves and take advantage of their employees' wages. Capitalist societies also face the weakness of discrimination and bias in job interviews, which prevent able and more superior people being given the job over someone who is inferior to them based on the employers biased taste. It is a sad fact that in societies today, when there is a shortage of jobs, a person is forced to live on benefits if available which is disgusting. It is an even more annoying that the people who don't actively seek jobs also gain the benefits.

People should be encouraged to seek jobs, through the means of controlling young people's career's following their departure from education and offering all the potential options that the person would be good at, and more importantly, is interested in. If they don't pursue any of the offers, then they should be forced to live under Class 4 (see Chapter 2), and as a sort of punishment to them and to make them regret turning down the offers; discrimination towards these people won't be as closely monitored or dealt with as strictly as it would otherwise be with higher class levels.

Because Capitalist societies rely on currency, when there is an economic crisis and the government itself is in trouble, people lose benefits and therefore the whole guarantee of benefits and the minimum wage is centred on the economy, and therefore currency. Because of the government's reliance on the economy, many people starve to death in countries that are poor, backward and overpopulated. Many people end up in life never getting a job they like, and are therefore miserable and stressed their entire working life. Therefore inequality cannot be addressed if the state hasn't got control of all businesses because discrimination and racism silently occur in the workforce and when applying for jobs in a privatised Capitalist society.

Also in Capitalist societies, especially the corrupt ones like India and the Far East, as well as many Eastern European countries now; there is simply too much of a gap between the poor and the rich. Some hard-working people in corrupt Capitalist countries like India live on ridiculous amounts of money like 50pence a week, while at the top of a scale you have multi-billionaires who do nothing but bathe in their money all day and brag about it to everyone in their fast multi-million pound cars. If you have any common sense, you would know that Humans, as a species, aren't this far apart from each other individually. Sure, there are others who are more intelligent than others, but even if the most stupid person in the world was living on hardly anything, while the most successful had unlimited amount of money, it still wouldn't be right. In states with a currency, there should instead be at least a firm limit on the amount of money a person lives off, one that's at least more equal and fair.

Privatised Capitalist countries businesses also make a profit by adding hefty price tags that amount to more than what they were bought for. The result is that due to currency, the privatised Capitalist businesses charge more than what the value of the product is, ultimately increasing the gap between the rich who can afford the items, and the poor who can't.

The Capitalist world would be justifiable if the rich people actually deserved the amount of money they have, but in most cases, especially in corrupt countries, they simply don't do anything for their country and are some of the most ignorant people in the world, because they think they can do anything because their billionaires; thinking they can just bribe the police to get away with crimes. Fines against the rich are useless, as £5000 is nothing to them, therefore people like Justin Bieber need to be punished by other means. A lot of the extremely rich have their money inherited from a long line of family members, which isn't right, in all fairness, if that person is mentally disabled, completely dependent on others, does nothing to contribute to their country or is otherwise a criminal. There could be a really successful, rich person who inherits his money to his friends or family, or shares his money with them while still alive and they could be complete idiotic, selfish people. Therefore, once again, it is another point in why money should be eradicated and be replaced with wealth classes and the government should have control over young people's future after they leave school.

Under Distributism, all people who have finished with education will immediately go directly to a State official, who will assess the individual's educational results and interests, and then present them with a list of job options and their class level based on their educational level. Jobs given to the young person should prioritise the person's interest and general educational strengths. Also by having state control over jobs, the government can take full advantage of the areas of the economy that need to be distributed more evenly and can therefore adapt to differing situations over time by distributing jobs to its workforce.

In this way, people will theoretically be guaranteed a job, and if they choose not to take any, they will still be guaranteed food under Class 4, which will eliminate all poverty which is so common in corrupt, Capitalist societies who have a low minimum wage, no benefits or a shortage of jobs due to their reliance on currency and private enterprise. Often greedy business owners employ the minimum amount of workers as a strategy so they can get the maximum amount of money, which is good for them, but by doing this it does greatly deteriote the general stability of the business and the appeal to consumers. On a wider scale it also makes jobs harder to come by for everyone seeking jobs. Capitalist societies are the embodiment of human greed, contributing to the widening gap between the rich and the poor.

Communism and Socialism's weakness' are that though they reduce inequality, they simply reduce it too much. By having people being paid the same for everything, it eliminates ones purpose to work harder for something, and therefore some workers will eventually stop working and become lazy, because they will know they will get paid anyway, and a revolution would occur. It is similar to Karl Marx's theory of how the industrial workers will rise up against the business owners, just the opposite. Everyone should know by now Humans aren't perfect, unfortunately people make errors, mistakes and they each have their own individual weaknesses. There are many who don't work as hard as their fellow colleges for the same amount of money. Instead in Socialist societies where everyone is paid the same, many will just take advantage of this, and stop working as hard as a lot of people, therefore causing a sense of inequality again despite everyone being paid the same. The Industrial workers will instead rise up against the unfair work effort of other work colleges and protest against Socialist economic equality.

So the workers strikes against Socialism will halt industrial production and therefore damage the fragile economy, resulting in the Socialist government having to lower workers' wages, which will cause complete outrage. The Socialist and Communist and all other ideologies reliance on currency doesn't do any wonders for them, because the economy can still be damaged by the stoppage of industrial production and strikes, Socialism and Communism won't therefore be completely safe from an economic crisis. That is why it is vitally important to eliminate currency first, before Socialism can overall, be in any way moderately successful.

The general population needs will be fulfilled by the state control of young people's careers, industry will boom in the right way the government would want it to by Distributing all the important sectors of the economy first, which is impossible to do in a Capitalist state because of private enterprise. With the use of wealth classes, the economy won't fall apart due to an economic crisis as there won't be a form of currency, the only way the economy would be able to collapse under a Distributist government therefore would be if industrial production comes to a halt, which won't happen because the government will be able to satisfy nearly every individual's idealistic job.

On the plus side, Communism has the right idea of enforcing total state control of business, for the reasons mentioned above, as it prevents the major faults of Capitalism from damaging the minds of the people, by stopping racism in job applications that superior people would of otherwise have received. Of course, the Communist reason to enforce state control was for a slightly different reason, it was mainly to stop private businesses from paying people different amounts of money. The other thing the Communists got right was collectivisation, though perhaps not in the ideal way a Distributist government would do it. The Communists governments' weren't really that bothered with rapidly draining peasants of their resources, even if it meant famine. Examples include Mao Zedong's failed 'Great Leap Forward' programme in which 30 million Chinese died and Stalin's rapid collectivisation of peasant's crops. The difference is the Distributist government prioritises the feeding of her population as first and also when needed, ideally puts a restriction on population level and effectively controls the population level.

The Liberalist view that people should have the most freedom as possible and to minimise state control, for the same reasons as Socialism, is flawed. Liberalism, whilst it would be better for the general freedom of an individual, by eradicating state control the nation would simply sweep into anarchy and social unrest, caused by corrupt businessmen who own large business. The restriction of laws and order in the Liberalist sense will therefore encourage crime rates as well as corruption, if the Liberalists stick with Capitalism. In general, though, without enforcement of psychopaths the state would simply dissolve into anarchy, people would think they can do what they like and the overthrowment of the Liberalist government would occur, by the people who are subjected to the abuse of petty criminals and anarchists. Then the state would henceforth become an Anarchist and cease to be a country. All business will be destroyed, production will stop, and technology would go back to the Stone Age due to the lack of development and available jobs caused by 'free people', who would expect everyone else to take care of a fragile economy.

The rapid industrialisation that was prioritised by the likes of Leon Trotsky and Joseph Stalin is to an extent flawed, as we now know that by having too much factories has a negative effect on the Earth's atmosphere, helping pollution take effect. However, it is of course necessary to have sufficient industry to have the minimum requirements to attain near complete self-sufficiency, in case of nuclear fallout. Therefore, to have a large industry and at the same time stopping pollution in populated areas, factories should mostly be built in the acquired to-be Arctic oversea territories, where Britain's inhabitants and also land animals are seldom seen, due to in part of the cold weather. Other ways round this is to enforce renewable and clean energy which will not damage the Earth's atmosphere.

By eliminating currency, then people will no longer be governed by a note which controls their lives and instead the economy will be a free economy, Distributing all the state resources to feed the population as top priority, with the wealth classes requirements as second and using the remaining resources to construct buildings and vehicles. If the world continues to go by Capitalist way, and doesn't address the effects of global warming, pollution and overpopulation, then their systems of government will collapse, likely in a devastating nuclear war.

First, there will be a AI (Artificial Intelligence) Revolution where millions of people in non-Distributist countries will lose their jobs to relentless, superior machines who don't have to be paid. Then, the economy as we know it will collapse due to unemployment, the unemployed will rise up against the machines and demand the return of their jobs and the banning of the machines, which the greedy business owners of the Capitalist world would be reluctant to do, due to Humans having to be paid.

At this stage, the global food shortages and dramatic rising prices caused by overpopulation and unemployment respectively will intensify the uprisings, many in overpopulated countries will eventually starve to death due to being unemployed or being paid too little to keep up with food prices. Even some of the wealthy will have some food shortages, due to climate change rendering warm countries crops infertile, the extinction of many animals, the economic sanctions countries will impose on some dependent economies which will hamper trade and rising sea levels which will in the process will destroy farming land and settlements.

The next stage, of course would be war. Countries relying on currency and not taking climate changes seriously will be under enormous pressure from their people to invade a weaker country, for food and resources. At this point in the future (likely somewhere from 2040-2080) more countries will have nuclear weapons, some will use these weapons in a relentless, unprovoked attack against a country with a lot of resources, and therefore cause the country to collapse before retaliation can take place. Nuclear war will probably happen after the stronger countries invade the weaker ones though, as the stronger countries will need the cultivatable land of the countries uncontaminated with radiation to feed the country's population, which would be their goal in the first place. The weaker countries will likely retaliate with nuclear weapons if they had access to them though. Nonetheless huge death tolls would occur in a moderately long World War, even if it is largely nuclear-free.

Then there would be the problem of enforcing control over the conquered, starving people. Likely the struggling imperialist, capitalist nations will extract all the resources from the invaded countries and ship them back to their own country and then, the stronger country, due to the threat of aggression from the conquered people or the weaker countries resentment of starvation, one of them will launch a nuclear attack against one another. It is likely the one who launches it first will bombarded the enemy with relentless nuclear bombs all at the same time, destroying the country before retaliation can take place.

The Distributist countries will prevail unhindered from a devastating war, there will be no riots due to food prices, no food shortages providing they have vertical farms, protecting the land through the use of barriers across the borders and controls the population to a manageable level. Distributist military's will be able to protect them from the hostile, starving non-Distributist countries, with the use of extensive anti-missile defence systems. So in the end, all Capitalist, Communist and all other non-Distributist countries will fall while the Distributist countries will take the leadership of the world, now at a stable level due to the destruction caused by a catastrophic nuclear war.

Chapter 7

Culture in a Distributist-run Britain

Under Distributism, the state's culture will be quite different compared to today's society in Britain. Because of the absence of currency, there won't be such a broad spectrum of prosperity, prosperity being divided into four classes, whom everyone will come under. In life, youngsters coming out of education will instead of everyday worrying about the economy and them getting the sack and then being unable to find jobs, they will have their future automatically given to them by the state itself once finished education, they will be guaranteed a job of some sort, and every individual should always get multiple job opportunities based on their strengths and interests in education. The days of overwhelming stress and anxiety will go under a system which will guarantee someone a job and a class level which even under class 4 guarantees them basic human rights such as food and shelter, unlike some poor countries with currency. People will live their lives in this regard happier, due to the stability of the Distributist system, not burdened by fears of economic depression, underpayment and corruption, and over-taxing of governments.

There will still be prosperity gap between those who deserve it and those who don't, though, perhaps not as extreme as most Capitalist countries in 2015. The gap ranges from the Class 4 people, the unemployed and immigrants who've been in the country for less than 3 years and Class 1, who tend to be celebrities, high-ranking government officials, high-ranking military officials and people who are in charge of a large business. Class 4 civilians will be far better-off than poor people in many parts of Africa, though they will still live in relatively poor conditions as a form of justice and response to their dismissal of a job opportunity in the first place. They will live in small, but reasonably adequate apartments. The bulk of Class 4 civilians will live in cities, in extremely tall skyscraper apartments built to accommodate as many Class 4 civilians as possible into a single building. Class 4 people will have a very limited sense of present culture, individuals limited to just one set of clothes, having no access to movies, video games or televisions. Class 4 people will still be able to keep up to date with the news via the internet through a mobile phone as well as YouTube and many other things available on the Internet. To encourage Class 4 people to seek a career, mild discrimination against them should be accepted.

The Class 1 people on the other side of the spectrum will have large-mansion sized homes, customised to their preference, options of a caretaker, the best cars, their full choice of any meal (providing it is under the national daily food intake allowance), extremely large quantities of entertainment choices, a large garden, up to 2 bodyguards and exotic pets. Class 1 citizens, like Class 4 citizens; should take up a very small percentage of the population. Unlike the multi-pound billionaires at present, Class 1 citizens shouldn't have massive yachts, their own aircraft and multiple houses. Work associated with money such as art, valuable books and also animal products should be housed inside a museum. The gap between the rich and the poor shown by the staggering difference in statistics will be gone, which shall boost the average person's morale in any case.

With the exception of Class 4, all classes will get equal amounts of food, determined by ounces. Food for all classes should be delivered once a week, the higher you're class level is, the more food options with better quality people should have. Restaurants will still exist, people will still be employed there as an integral part of the workforce. Restaurants themselves and all other businesses are to be controlled by the state itself to eliminate corruption and enforce Distributist control. On the road, vehicles will range from the slow, uncomfortable and dull-looking Class 3 cars and the luxurious supercars and 380hp 5 litre V8 Limos of Class 1. Class 4 will be limited to coaches and taxis as a means of travel.

Class 3 cars should be having no interior luxuries such as leather, wood, thick chairs, arm rests, spaciousness or thick windows. Tyres should be thin and heavily grooved and wheels should be plain and dull-looking. Colours should be limited to urine yellow, lime green, pink, brown, white, grey and bright orange. Vehicles have no more than 160bhp, no modifications, no lightweight parts, no traction control, no power steering and a suspension height of over 150mm. Class 3 styling should be bland and dull; no grilles, no fancy headlights, no aerodynamic attachments, basic door handles and no prominent wheel arches. An ideal Class 3 car would be something like a heavily outdated Honda Civic, Renault Twingo or a second generation (1979-1983) Honda Civic, or alternatively for one person only; a Peel P50. As everything will be nationalised under Distributism, the British government should design and put forward ideas for new mass-produced cars for specific classes.

Class 2 vehicles can include vehicles which have up to 400bhp, mild modifications, a suspension height of over 90mm, some lightweight parts, traction control, ABS, power steering, grilles, good lights, prominent wheel arches, some aerodynamic attachments, grilles, more choice of colours, leather, spaciousness, luxury and thicker furniture. Class 1 vehicles can have virtually anything, as long as they have under 1,500bhp (which should be classified as illegal on public roads).

Miscellaneous cars such as taxi's, police cars and ambulances should all be completely state-produced. Like I mentioned in chapter 5, police cars should be comparatively fast to catch criminals. All police cars should be powered by a 4.0 litre supercharged V8 petrol engine producing 360bhp. 0-100 should come under 15 seconds and top speed should be over 150mph. Ambulances should also be much faster so they can get to hospitals on time in desperate situations; they should be powered by a 2.0 litre turbocharged V6 petrol engine producing 280bhp. Taxis should be as fuel efficient as possible; a 1.6 litre straight 4 diesel engine producing 100bhp would be plenty for Class 4 transport.

Festivals should be an important part of lifestyle, different festivals should be held every day of the week during the night. All classes should be permitted to attend the festivals except Class 4. Festivals purpose in a Distributist society will be to purely entertain people and serve an important daily event. All festivals should be held at a stadium, which should be built and based on Rome's Coliseum which was successful in holding events for centuries. Stadiums in Towns of 50,000 people should be 70ft tall, in cities of 250,000 people, 300ft tall, large cities (762m) and London 3,200m which accommodates 7 million people or 100,000 per 150ft. London's stadium, due to its sheer size and capacity, will be a highly valued landmark for tourists during the day, while at evening and night serving its purpose as an event holder. The London coliseum will also feature the Distributist leader's seat and spectating position, as well as the British royal family and 7 seats for the National Council members. All festivals will have bars and cafe's to eat at.

On Monday's an adult sex and social festival should be held, it will be primarily for the single people 18 and over. The Monday sex festival should be held from 20:00 until midnight. People engaging in Monday's festival should be encouraged to have as much sex as possible, bonding and becoming friends with people in the process. Monday's festival will be a good display of the newfound 'cultural openness' of Britain. Although elsewhere in public, full nudity will be classed as a small crime, Monday's sex festival will be an exception; it will instead be compulsory for everyone participating to be naked.

Monday's festival, then, would be a chance once a week for people to show their devotion or feelings towards people of the opposite sex.

Clothing should be more traditional in the sense of a general difference between males and females. Advertisements should always feature women in dresses or alternatively mini-skirts. The production and manufacturing of female clothing should therefore be focused on dresses and skirts. Female trainers should be outlawed; instead feminine shoes, boots and high-heels should be fully focused on. The dying of hair should also be banned, in order to give women a more natural look. Clothing, like cars; should also be available to certain class levels only, in order to replace the Capitalist system of currency in a way which isn't as severe and can be fully controlled. For instance, certain clothing materials and exotic designs should only be legally available for the higher class levels. Police officers, health care specialists, state officials and government members should all be expected to wear a type of suit best accustomed to their job. Men's clothing in general should be smarter and slightly more formal than it is today.

Tuesday's festival should be a gladiator-themed battle. Matches will involve two men fighting each other with wooden swords for a maximum of 10 minutes. The maximum number of participants entering the tournament should be restricted to 60, to fit in the time. Victory is consolidated when one man is knocked down and unable to get up after a ten count, like a boxing match. If both people fight until the end of the time limit, then victory is determined by scorecards by five judges on scores of 100. The winner of the tournament has to survive an encounter with a Bengal Tiger for a minute to be crowned champion. The champion doesn't have to participate in the next tournament, but has to defend the championship against the winner of the next tournament providing they survive the encounter with the tiger. The champion can keep on defending against tournament winners until he loses or he decides to retire from Gladiator fights after a minimum of 5 defences.

Thus a serious and fierce individual will have to take in mind that they will have to take part in at least another 5 matches with a formidable opponent over the course of five weeks until they can decide to 'throw in the towel'. Champion's trophies include a bottle of champagne, a gold cup studded with diamonds and a sword crafted to the champions liking. The champions keep the gold cup/trophy and the sword as a permanent reminder of themselves being former gladiatorial champions. A champion has to defend the championship successfully at least three times before they are granted their sword, though. This would be necessary to encourage champions to defend the championship to obtain the sword as well as more prestige.

The militarisation of young men will be an important part of the culture of a Distributist society. From the age of 18, following their departure from education, all boys should be enlisted in the military for six months as part of conscription. Actual male military personnel who serve in the military as a job should have it compulsory to maintain a moustache or thick sideburns in an attempt to make military forces more intimidating to foes and to differentiate the Distributist forces from the foreign military forces. Compulsory facial hair should only apply to active/full-time military personnel. Also, men who achieve the rank of sergeant or lieutenant in the British Army should get a compulsory tattoo of the British flag and the flag of their regiment. High-ranking soldiers of the RAF and the Royal Navy should also get similar tattoos. The men participating in gladiator battles of Tuesday's festival will be an important part in introducing young men into a more military-orientated lifestyle. Boxing matches should be held in schools and colleges, and recruitment posters should be commonplace in city centre buildings. Even people in non-military jobs such as bricklayers and plumbers should be valued for their fitness as well as skill.

Wednesday's festival should be circus-themed with a prominent firework display. Entertainment should appeal to all age groups; there being game prizes to children's liking and adults. At least 10% of the festival's population should be professional clowns, doing all kinds of tricks and jokes that appeal to all audiences. Examples of some games should be Five Finger Fillet, Equilibristics, Juggling, Jumping, Globe of Death, Fortune Teller, Mad Houses, Mazes, roller coasters, trampolines and the Wheel of Death. Other attractions should also include animals such as elephants, monkeys, ponies, unique people and various shocking bodily acts.

Thursday's festival should be an alcohol-based festival, where everyone participating in the festival basically has as many drinks as they like from 19:00 until midnight. Age limits require people to be at least 16 years old to consume alcohol. Entertainment should include DJ's, pole-dancers, lap-dancing, quizzes, dartboards, pool tables, board games and gambling (in the form of prizes). During Thursday's festival, local pool, dart, chess, blackjack, monopoly and trivia championships should be held like Tuesday's gladiatorial championship. For obvious reasons, security during Thursday's event should be tripled than those of other festivals.

Friday's festival is to be a historical festival; each Friday the historical period will change. The week's marked historical period will result in the festival being themed around that specific time frame, people having to dress in the appropriate manner for the time period to participate in the festival. Time periods should include the 11th century, the late and early Victorian eras, an Ancient Rome-themed festival, a prehistoric festival, the 18th, 17th and 16th centuries as well as the most prominent decades of the 20th century. These historical festivals should be immaculate, to the extent of believing you've travelled back in time to the certain time period. All participants should also be encouraged to act like as if they were from the time period as well. If available, vintage newspapers from the time period should be represented to participants of the festival and actors playing historical figures should also be taken into consideration. Friday's festival will start at 9:00 and finish at 23:00.

Architecture will go through a revolution; buildings which aren't tall enough or big enough for Distributist standards should be scrapped or otherwise added on too. Buildings which hold a certain degree of heritage and historical value should be left untouched and restored to their original condition when needed such as various historical castles, the Houses of Parliament, Tower Bridge, the Shard, London Eye and various historical and stunning cathedrals and churches.

In urban areas, large city centres specifically specialising in one interest should be built in order to make things easier to find for pedestrians. Some of the city centres which could be built would be research centres, shopping centres, restaurant centres 'Standard' churches should be 100ft tall and cathedrals 500ft tall to accommodate all local religious worshipers into one building. Schools should be about 100ft tall, colleges 120ft and universities 700 metres tall. New Distributist buildings should be expressed through the merging of the finest Gothic and Futuristic architectural styling. Places of worship and other buildings which house ancient teachings should be Gothic in style, whilst military barracks and prison/labour camps should be Ancient-looking; the military barracks and the London Labour Camp being crafted out of stone, and the rest of the Labour Camps in the north of the Empire being made of limestone blocks or alternatively concrete. Schools, city centres and other buildings home to work, in a perfect contrast, should be futuristic in style.

Automotive garages should be 60ft tall; in order to have multiple floors of cars for better usage of land mass. The height of other standard buildings are as follows: theatres (100ft), research centres (400ft), shopping centres (1,000ft), restaurant centres (900ft), museums (700ft), libraries (150ft), town apartments (300ft), city apartments (1,200ft), large city apartments (2,000ft) and industrial factories 850ft tall and a width and depth of 500ft to make space for the large industrial equipment and machines.

London itself shall become the first supercity, due to its immensely tall buildings. The Palace of Westminster will be reserved for a tourist attraction; the 2,000 metre tall State Council of Ministers building will be at the centre of London which would be the residence of National Council members, the Emperor and other high-ranking politicians. Local churches in the suburbs of London will be enlarged to 150ft tall, and a London University will be a major landmark at 1,600m tall. London will also be home to four 1,000m tall museums, including an enlarged British Museum, Natural History Museum and Science Museum as well as an Art Museum. Other important attractions will include a 350ft tall London Motor Centre and a 1,100m tall Research Centre where the top scientific projects will take place using the best scientists. Due to the increased high-rise buildings in a Distributist society, automation research such as quicker elevators should be researched miraculously.

Saturday's festival will be a music based festival. Local bands will gather and put on performance between 18:30 and 22:00, with London featuring the best bands from the UK. Activities that weren't otherwise completed on Thursday's festival would be continued on Saturday. Sunday's festival is to be primarily a kids-based festival, featuring attractions for people aged between the years of 3-15 years of age.

The London Labour Camp should be displayed to Londoners in a manner in a way to shock and frighten onlookers. Only in London, the only labour camp in mainland Britain will have public executions. Public executions should be reserved for terrorists and other enemies of the state only. The London Labour Camp's appearance alone should be enough to fill the average person with dread, as would the prisoners working on making products relentlessly outside. Elsewhere in populated areas of the British Empire, pictures and posters depicting life in a labour camp should be scattered about on buses, streets, buildings and attractions. On some TV channels, adverts depicting life in a labour camp should also be used. The purpose of this would be to mentally destroy a person's criminal thoughts in regards to their will in committing a crime, in an attempt to significantly lower crime attempts.

Religiously, Britain will be perhaps the most diverse nation in regards to religion on the planet, as cathedrals and churches will be extremely divergent; housing multiple religions in the same building. Islam will be banned, and Muslims from Britain will be forcefully removed, due to reasons explained in Chapter 1. Religion itself will become the most peaceful cultural aspect of a Distributist society, as children will be brought up in a manner which is respectful of different religions. Religion therefore will cease to be a belief associated with war, and instead be intended for one of the most cultural connection between British people in a Distributist society. Like most religions originally intended to be, all religions will be peaceful. Entertainment such as film, literature and art especially, should be mainly focused on the triumph of Distributism over all the other weak political ideologies which rely on currency. In art, a feature that would be significantly respected would be art works that express how great Distributism is, and expresses the important ideologies of Distributism.

Chapter 8

Raasism

Raasism, pronounced rar-sism is the alternative name for permanent Distributist revolution. The non-Distributist states may fall much earlier than expected; economic investigators have forecasted that the United States economy will crash towards the end of 2016. Reasons which may intensify the crash include the over-use of imported materials and the limited selling of exports ($1.64 trillion exports sold in 2014 and $2.37 trillion imported items) and a public debt of 102% of GDP.

Of course, if the US does end up in a severe financial crisis over the next few years, the consequences will be disastrous for the whole world. The Wall Street Crash of October 1929 had disastrous consequences for the rest of the world, starting the Great Depression. Some investigators say it is to be even worse than the Great Depression, which if correct will cause the population living in poverty in Britain to rise from the already-bad statistic of 16.6% to possibly 40%. With the Tories in power, the statistic will likely go to 40%. The Conservatives, having unfairly won the majority of votes after the UKIP party only got 1 seat despite having more votes than the Liberal Democrats and the Scottish Nationalists combined; will continue to wreak havoc on the United Kingdom. David Cameron and his devious team of rich slobs will increase interest rates and taxes drastically; widening the gap between rich and poor to disastrous levels and isolate the middle class.

With practically all the MPs not actually wishing to come out of the EU, the 2017 EU membership referendum's results will therefore be likely duplicated to the Conservative-dominated parliament desires, just like how they dictated the UKIP Party's MP candidates in the 2015 general election. Thus, with the EU membership's dissolution in this sense being bound to be largely unachievable, the mass immigration will continue and the number of terrorists in the UK will rise like breeding rats. Regardless of whether the 2017 economic crash will happen, the Conservatives will certainly increase the population living below the poverty line with their increased taxes, interest rates and general higher costs of living. At 16.6% below the poverty line in the UK, makes the UK one of the worst in the Europe. Some of these people don't pursue jobs and therefore deserve it; but others genuinely are just unlucky at finding a job with the shortages there are today. Perhaps by the end of their term, the Conservatives may have over 20% living in poverty even if we aren't pulled into another economic crisis.

With the increased private enterprise of the world, global recession's possibility of happening has increased tenfold since the end of the Cold War. With the increasing number of people as well, combined with the growing job shortages thus contribute to the growing number of people living in poverty. Also global warming will continue to disrupt economic stability with rising sea levels, growing temperatures, pollution and wildlife extinction rates. With housing prices miraculously going up much faster than people's wages, and vacant houses standing derelict, house prices will help plunge young people into homelessness thanks to banking. Also, food prices and the general costs of living go up faster than the lower class can manage, thanks to the shortage of certain animals, the growing population of the world and the worrying shortages of oil.

Also, of course, the growing number of people also means that there is more of a chance of a financial crisis, with more people spending money they don't have and borrowing too much will trigger debts to become increasingly unpayable to banks. The banks will in turn boost prices to disastrous levels, which had caused the 2008 financial crisis.

An economic crash that could plunge the US and the rest of the world into poverty though could happen for a different reason. An American war with Russia would likely involve the EU if it was to happen and a WW3-inducing scenario could trigger world economic collapse due to nuclear fallout, worker casualties and crop destroying. Vladimir Putin, the leader of Russia; will clearly stop at nothing to get what he wants such as Crimea. Putin probably has bigger ambitions than Crimea though; he may want to restore former Soviet and Russian Empire territories of Ukraine, the Baltic States, Belarus, Georgia and even Poland. Ukraine holds 17% of Russians within their population, Latvia 26% and Estonia 24%. Putin may also wish to conquer the lands if the Baltic states of Lithuania, Latvia and Estonia to be united with Kaliningrad. Ukraine in particular, was also the lands of the ancient Russian people, known as Kievan Rus which was established in 882AD and was dismantled by the Mongol invasion around 1240. Kiev was the historical capital of the ancient Russian people and continued to be a strong principality well into the 14th century and then later came under Russian influence in later centuries after breakup of the Golden Horde.

Individual states within the European Union are still in trouble from the horrors of the 2008 financial crisis. Greece is still suffering from severe unemployment (25% unemployed) and mass poverty rates of over 30%. They aren't receiving hardly any help from EU member states which shows just how useless the EU really is, Germany's Chancellor Angela Merkel refusing to pay WWII reparations to Greece. Cyprus is struggling from a similar situation and Spain hasn't fully recovered at all from the financial crash. The four main powers of Europe (Germany, UK, France and Italy) have economies which are suffering from extremely low growth compared to states such as Vietnam, China and India.

The UK economy is a service-dominated economy, services taking up nearly 80% of the labour forces occupation. The more EU members who are still in financial chaos will increase their chances of leaving the European Union, which will in turn hamper the UK's trade with the former-EU states to an extent. The industrial resources Britain gets from the EU whom she desperately needs to survive could result in material shortages and possible food rationing.

Thus a financial crash which succeeds in decreasing EU membership may have disastrous consequences for the UK. As mentioned in chapter 1, this doesn't mean I've changed my thoughts about EU membership. The UK needs to be self-sufficient for Distributism to work; otherwise it would mean chaotic results for the United Kingdom. That means coming out of the EU, and then miraculously starting a huge industrial and agricultural remapping of the British economy which would ideally be distributed to a minimum percentage of the UK work force to retain a good service sector and to decrease chances of surplus materials. Britain is where Distributism originated; thus probably will be the first state to become Distributist. The states with currency will think of Distributism like Capitalist states viewed Communist USSR after 1917 and cease to have diplomatic relations and trade with Britain.

Ideally, Britain needs to be reasonably self-sufficient enough before isolationism and full Distributist rule is implemented so the United Kingdom doesn't starve in the months and possible years of development of the farms needed for food sufficiency. Also, Britain needs to be transformed into an industrial powerhouse by colonising Greenland, Antarctica and possibly Iceland before foreign relations are terminated so the British people have the products promised to them by their respective class level. Thus, the UK will probably have to rely on currency and its Capitalist partners' exports for a while until decent sufficiency has been accomplished.

To help increase the chances of Distributist revolution in foreign states, a Raasist Union should be established. The Raasist Union should have its own online website where Distributist supporters from all over the world can show their support, ask questions and help spread revolution to their individual countries. Distributist flags and military equipment should be sold to the members of the website, where upon buying they can exercise Distributist revolution in their living area. To become a member, individuals will have to go through a political ideology quiz to determine whether they themselves fit in with Distributist ideology. If the individual successfully completes the quiz after no more than two turns, then they should be awarded Raasist Union membership.

As the 2015 general elections showed clearly, a non-Labour or non-Conservative government will never get into power through the poor current system of elections. Distributist rule can therefore only be realistically achieved through successful revolution. Alternatively, the Distributist leader in Britain could attempt to win the monarchs approval and support for establishing a one-party state like Benito Mussolini had done in October 1922 in the 'March on Rome'. Option B would be the most preferable, as it would be won through non-violence.

To members and non-members alike, the site should have copies of 'A New Ideology' for sale and the main basic ideologies of Distributism available to non-members. More detailed articles on Distributist interpretation on various subjects should be available to Raasist Union members. Social networking sites should also have a multi-cultural Raasist Union page. All states with a Raasist presence should have their own national Distributist headquarters and their own leader. All Raasist leaders in their own specific countries should have immense respect for the British Distributist leader and later, British Emperor. Raasist leaders should be elected as leader by votes of the national Distributist party and then the winner should be approved by the British Distributist leader. Foreign states that should have a Raasist presence include: Russia, Ireland, the United States, Italy, France, Spain, Norway, Canada, Greece, non-Arab African states, Iceland, Japan, Australia, New Zealand, Papua New

Guinea and all East European states excluding Ukraine and Belarus.

In desperate circumstances, dictators such as Kim-Jong-Un of North Korea could be approached with the Distributist ideology. The Japanese economy is actually shrinking, poverty is at 16% and public debt is 226% of GDP. The Japanese Raasist leader can promote that a Distributist government will eradicate all debts caused by currency, eradicate poverty, replace working hours with a more fairer wealth class system (as Japanese workers are extremely stressed compared to the west due to high working hours) and also perhaps revive Japanese imperialism. I consider the Japanese to be the most advanced Asian people, being a major developer of video gaming, machines and computing. To have a Distributist Japanese government with a strong leader would be powerful ally.

The Spanish Raasist leader could also promise to eradicate all debts amounting to 92% of GDP with a superior class system, to reduce unemployment to fewer than 5% and to lead a much more decisive government with a revival of Spanish colonialism on islands across the Atlantic and Latin America and to come out of the EU.

The French Raasist leader could criticise the EU and turn the French people against the EU for being a secret Nazi idea, and that Germany's real motive is to invade France again. They could further criticise the EU for allowing the Islamification of France take its hold, as over six million Muslims are in France as of 2015. The French Raasist leader could also condemn currency for its weak and un-growing economy. French nationalists could also be appeased greatly by building up the French military, the eradication of

Muslims from France and the potential aid in helping the British destroy terrorism in the Middle East. After the British and French have destroyed terrorism in the Middle East, then the French should colonise Syria and Iraq as part of reviving the French Empire.

The Italian Raasist leader could criticise currency for low economic growth and convince the Vatican that Islam is plotting to take over the world religiously, which is in effect; what the Islamic terrorist groups are actually trying to do and rule the world under a brutal Islamic dictatorship. This is significant as it is true, Islamic extremists wanting to eradicate all other false idols and religions, as evidenced by ISIL's ideology and their prompt destruction of ancient relics in the Middle East. The Italian Raasist leader could then further criticise the EU for forcing illegal immigrants coming into Italy in cargo ships and pledge to build Italy into a superpower.

In African states, the Raasist Union states there will probably be the most successful. African Raasist leaders could exploit the tremendous gap between the starving poor and the filthy rich and promise to reduce the gap significantly, with the state controlled wealth class government-dictating system which will ultimately make society a much fairer and successful place if done right. Other African Raasist leader's policies should include the modernisation of the state, and all the Distributist ideologies.

East European states' leaders should have extremely nationalist policies and a deep sense of resentment to Russia's territorial size and territorial ambitions. This would be necessary internationally to prevent Russia from ever becoming too powerful or rather, too large. Also East European Raasist leaders could possibly hold the theory that Germany and the EU is still secretly run by Nazi's and that they are working with Muslims (which Hitler had preferred to Christianity as the main religion in Germany) to conquer the world and kill all Jews, starting with Eastern Europe as Hitler had done as part of his Lebensraum policy.

Greece's Raasist leader should greatly despise the EU and currency for plunging them into a financial crisis and not helping them. The wealth class system will promise to give the 34% of people in poverty housing accommodations and sufficient food. The Greek Raasist leader could also talk of an imminent invasion from the south east from Muslim countries, promising to help France and Britain eradicate Islam. The Greek Raasist leader could also talk of reviving the Ancient Greek Empire; conquering Balkan territories and Cyprus and expanding eastwards to Turkey.

The United States Raasist leader, in contrast to other Raasist leaders; should support anarchy and general chaos of the United States in an effort to weaken the United States superpower-status. US intelligence groups such as the CIA and the FBI make actual Distributist rule unlikely, as the CIA and FBI will no doubt attempt to dissolve the American Distributist party before anything positive can happen. A similar scheme could be implemented in China.

All the Raasist leaders in English-speaking states should work to convince their country to become a part of the British Empire again. Although this may take time to happen, I feel that once the general people of Australia, Canada, New Zealand, Ireland and Papua New Guinea see how great the British government rule of the United Kingdom is, knowing the British will rule exactly the same with her colonies; it would be too tempting to resist to most people. These countries together will become part of the largest and most successful empire in human history. Norway and Iceland, despite not sharing the English language could easily be implemented into the British Empire due to Iceland's extremely low population and Norway's cold weather which makes Norway rely greatly on foreign imports, which under the British Empire will be free and in vast quantities; as well as its near location to Britain.

Four times a year, all high-ranking politicians of Raasist Union states should meet in Nuuk, capital of Greenland and discuss current world events and Distributist revolution worldwide. As part of their party symbol, all Raasist leaders symbol should be stylised as their own native country; with the Distributist colours of black, red and green replacing existing colours of their national flag.

If successful diplomatic annexation of the English-speaking countries doesn't occur within 75 years of the establishment of a Raasist leader in the specific state; then drastic actions should be taken. Providing the state doesn't have nuclear or other weapons of mass destruction; then a British force of 500,000 infantry troops, 4 Goliath airships, 16 submarines, 2,000 aircraft, 800 helicopters, 1,000 tanks, 4,000 artillery pieces and 19 destroyers should be sent to invade and colonise the English-speaking state. The Distributist party within the nation will tear the country apart from the inside whilst the formidable British force will invade it faultlessly from the outside. Citizens who oppose British rule should be prevented from rioting against the Empire, whilst keeping their freedom of speech and attitude towards British colonial rule. Once the Liberalists and the nationalists see how superior life will be like under the British Empire, then support for them will die down non-violently and the nationalists will in turn become British Empire nationalists. All the dominions should ideally be completely administered by the National Council in London, effectively run by the Emperor and Council members.

Nuclear weapons on the English-speaking states shouldn't be used in any situation, as the land will be useless and millions will die as a result of a nuclear attack. Also, support for the British Empire will die down due to the brutality of the attack. Non-hostile civilians shouldn't be harmed in any way and the British forces first priority should be to get to the capital and seize the government headquarters. In Britain and Ireland, former SNP politicians, Irish nationalists and their supporters should be kept under heavy surveillance by the police force to prevent them from potentially igniting a revolution which would be bad for everyone. Once colonialist people are introduced to the superior British government then there would be no need for nationalists and other political parties as a revolution would severely damage multiple countries and it would be very unlikely that the people striving for independence have a better political ideology than Distributism.

Also, all the English-speaking states were once apart of the British Empire and thus non-immigrants have British heritage from centuries back, where at one point in history their British ancestors crossed over to their English-speaking country. This is particularly true for Australia, New Zealand and Papua New Guinea. Asians now significantly populate Oceania, most coming from the overpopulated states of China, Japan and former-Indochina. Some of their ancestors came over to Oceania in the 19th century for gold mining and decided to stay there. I think it would be in the best interests of the British Empire, the native Aboriginals and the people in Oceania with European ancestry to eradicate the alien-race of Asians. The Asians whose family have been in Oceania for multiple generations should rightfully stay, whilst the Asians whose family have only come to Oceania in the past 50 years should be forced to go back to Asia.

There is no issue with simply gaining back territory which was Britain's before the 21st century. People of the Commonwealth must realise that 90% of their British ancestors would have wanted to keep the said territory under British rule. They still speak English, they look European and more importantly, their culture isn't much different from British people, despite being separated for centuries. For instance, in Australia, nothing is drastically different from the UK except the weather and the wildlife. Australia, New Zealand and Ireland share the United Kingdom's love of American Hollywood movies and TV programmes. Also in New Zealand and Australia particularly, Capitalism continues to value the rich over the poor in extreme levels. Half the population of New Zealand lives on less than $24,000 a year, whilst the richest 1% owns 16% of the country's wealth and the richest 5% own 38% of the country's wealth. Between 1982 and 2011, the average income of the richest 10% of New Zealand saw an increase from $56,000 to $100,000, whilst the poorest 10% only saw 13% increase.

All the English-speaking states mentioned were after-all, founded and colonised by a superior civilisation century's back, thus making Britain the rightful ruler of the colonies. A large and powerful empire is also above all, far more influential and powerful than a weak country. It can also be argued that the world would be more stable with a restored British Empire, as there will be less leaders and politicians in power to emerge and create wars, anti-Distributism and a general state of chaos.

As part of the British Empire, the desired English-speaking states will also get their items in a much more stable manner, as the large British Empire will be able to distribute her resources to all her colonies. Also, once quite a few major nations have become Distributist and cease to trade with states with currency; then this will in turn hurt the English-speaking states financially; in the empire colonies will all have multiple industrial specialities. Thus, by doing this all colonies in the empire will be dependent on each other for resources; if one colony strived for independence Britain and the rest of her colonies will have to fight to retain that colony under the British Empire as they would all need the specialised resources of the nationalist colony. After a few years of building up and distributing resources in the new dominions, one colony leaving the empire will have devastating consequences for the whole of the empire. The result is the greatest empire in history, at the pinnacle of stability thanks to dependence on each other to survive.

Britain in recent decades has been the target for terrorism and American Rulership. The British Armed Forces now only have 225,000 people and declining despite terrorism and the Ukraine crisis. This is hardly enough to be regarded as a 'Great Power'. Yes, we have nuclear weapons, though most are American-made and we have extremely low quantities of tanks and artillery compared to states such as Saudi Arabia and North Korea. The EU makes the UK a haven for terrorism thanks to uncontrolled illegal immigration to the UK, which the UN and the United States encourage.

Following the devastating Second World War Britain gradually lost its mighty empire which for centuries had produced many of Britain's raw materials. After Britain was de-ranked to Great Power status after the independence of India in 1947, the United States gradually grew closer to Britain for modern American imperialism or 'dollar imperialism' as it's known. Britain meanwhile grew even closer to America due to the Cold War and more importantly, the United Kingdom's dependence on US exports and financial aid which had its origins as far back as 1918 following the First World War when Europe began to rely on the leading economic superpower; the United States, for exports and had to pay large sums of reparations back from the Great War.

Since 1776, the United States has been at the forefront of the traitorous English-speaking colonies that turned their back on their Anglo-Saxon creators. Over the next century the US continued to make headlines with its growing wealth, overtaking Britain's Gross Domestic Power Purchasing Parity in 1870, becoming the richest nation on Earth when excluding the entire British Empire. In the next centuries, continuing now, the US has pushed and succeeded for the dominance of the English-speaking world.

The UK is now and has been since around the 1970's, effectively a 'mini America'. The United States following WW2 had backed the United Nations in enforcing peace and order in the world and has tried to dominate the world with its Capitalist ideology. Like the League of Nations was Britain and France's project, the United Nations is an American project to dictate the world in an American favour. British citizens can easily see this by looking at the world around them; a country now riddled and dominated by American movies, American TV and American technology. Evidence for the American support of the UN's 'Self-Determination' policy of all the European colonies following the Second World War, which ultimately was successful in aiding the pathetic nationalists for the independence of all Britain's major colonies; include the 1956 Suez Crisis, Woodrow Wilson's Self-Determination policy from 1919 and dozens of other former-British colonies who appealed to the US-backed United Nations for independence.

The UN and the United States were thereby responsible for the fragmentation of the British Empire which de-ranked Britain from global affairs. The 1956 Suez Crisis saw the United States and the UN condemn Britain and France for their old dying act of imperialist behaviour. This was actually a secret political tactic by the United States to finally bring about the destruction of the British Empire, so the United States was henceforth one step closer to dominating the world, becoming the undisputed leader of the English-speaking and Capitalist world. Under Distributist rule, Britain will become Great Britain again. Britain and all other territories of the British Empire will share the status as superpower and will be under the largest empire in history and the most powerful empire/country in the world. Upon successful Distributist revolution, the United States will cease to be a bully in disguise towards the United Kingdom and the glory days of the British Empire will be revived.

Under the British Empire millions of new jobs will be available, as all colonies of the empire will need supplies from other colonies; by way of cargo ships and aircraft. From Britain to Ireland to Iceland to Greenland to Antarctica to Australia, New Zealand and Papua New Guinea; a highly sophisticated travel network will make the transportation of resources throughout the British Empire rapidly indeed. The new empire jobs should be officially called 'Merchant Sailors' (the ones who deliver the empires goods by ship.) and 'Cargo Pilots' (the ones who deliver the empires goods by aircraft).

By 2100, the reformed British Empire should aim to have a combined population of 600 million inhabitants. Of the 600 million people; 1.8% of the labour force should be in the British armed forces and at least 7% of the labour forces should have scientific research-related jobs. Vertical farms should all be 1000ft tall and have 50 20ft tall floors with a total of 500 (or 10 per floor) farmers in a single vertical farm. Villages of 5,000 inhabitants should have a sole vertical farm whilst other settlements with higher populations should have their vertical farms multiplied. For instance a standard town of 50,000 people should have 10 vertical farms for itself. Total vertical farmers in the British Empire (2100) should be an estimated 50.526 million. In order to protect the integrity of the empire, the empires settlements' vertical farms should preferably be in different islands or continents so that particular settlement or perhaps country cannot simply choose to become independent.

The following ideological figures are how the empires resources or rather production should be distributed in her colonies once all the English-speaking states (excluding North America), are taken back as well as Greenland, Iceland and Antarctica in 2100:

Australia will become an industrial powerhouse, being the sole producer of the empire's lithium, iron, copper, gold, nickel, lead and livestock. Australia should also contribute to 60% of the empires magnesium produce, 50% of tin production, 20% of gas production, 10% of fishing occupations and 40% of aluminium production. The population of Australia should be significantly larger than it is now; with the vertical farms and high-rise living taken into account, the population of Australia should be at 40 million.

New Zealand will be the empire's vehicle manufacturer and up to 60% of the empire's building of industrial machines. New Zealand will also account for 3% of total oil produce, 40% of magnesium, 10% of geothermal power and 50% of tin production. Papua New Guinea will be the empire's sole producer of wood and silver production and 3% of total oil produce. The British Empire will also rely on the lush and beautiful country of Papua New Guinea for the manufacturing of construction materials which would be vital for the empire's high-rise settlements and 40% of fruit and vegetables.

Iceland will account for 60% of aluminium production, 20% of hydrogen, 25% of geothermal power, 5% of gas production, 4% of steel production and 40% of fishing occupants. Iceland will also be the empire's sole producer of ferrosilicon. Greenland will be the sole producer of uranium, tantalite and niobium. Greenland will also account for 30% of steel production, 35% of oil, 15% of gas, 40% of diamonds and 40% of fishing occupants. Antarctica should account for 40% of steel produce, 50% of oil, 60% of diamonds, 40% of hydrogen and 10% of gas.

Ireland will become the medical colony of the empire, manufacturing medical devices and being the sole producer of the empire's chemicals used in medicine. Ireland will also contribute to 30% of corn production, 25% of electricity, 15% of geothermal power, 10% of hydrogen, 20% of gas and 10% of fruit and vegetables. Britain, being the holder of the capital of the empire; should be responsible for the manufacturing of all scientific equipment, agricultural machines, defence equipment, educational equipment, all entertainment such as movies, games and books and the land where all the top scientific projects take place. Britain will also contribute to 30% of gas, 75% of electricity, 70% of corn, all hides, leather and game meat, 50% of fruit and vegetables, 50% of geothermal power, 9% of oil, 26% of steel output, 30% of hydrogen, 40% of industrial machines and 10% of fishing occupants. Britain will also be solely responsible for wheat, grain, and barley and rye production for alcohol fermentation.

Conclusion

It is important to analyse the superiority of the my Distributist regime over the United Kingdom and the United States in 2015. To refresh your memory, I will point out the principle aspects of the Distributist regime and express how it is superior to today's Capitalist society.

The usage of the wealth class system will establish a much more stable and fairer society, economic depression will be eliminated and by eliminating currency it would make it easier for the Distributist government to distribute the necessary resources promised to all classes more freely. Famine and poverty caused by economic collapse will be avoided, corrupt business owners will be eradicated, along with all the other disturbing things currency stands for, such as charging people unnecessarily. Houses will be put to full use instead of being stood derelict for years before they are purchased. Under a society not governed by currency and under government control, things can be built more easily and efficiently, workers wouldn't have to be paid and serious exploitation of Britain's resources can be fully implemented.

Under states with a national currency, I feel that currency is seriously holding back the progress of every country under a form of currency. Without currency, resources which aren't put to use due to economic budgets can be instead taken advantage of, the population can be controlled in order to manage the limited resources and recycling of materials will play a big factor in preserving materials for generations. This would result in a much more productive country at no cost, except of course resources, which if managed carefully and properly; with the population controlled, could do wonders for any country on Earth. In truth, Distributist states with a decent leader, advisors and loyal state officials, could save more resources than most countries today if done right.

Immigrants and terrorism will be suppressed by all means necessary; the control of the population will enable the government to properly manage resources. More usage of land will also take place with the tall office buildings, shopping malls, schools, factories, research stations and vertical farms, enabling more space and enough room for more citizens. UK Fauna will enjoy a much happier life than they are experiencing right now, more wildlife reserves and parks will be opened and established and roads will have short barriers across the outsides of them to prevent animal casualties from vehicles. The profit associated with animal products will be eradicated under a non-currency system, poachers and hunters will be in turn, eradicated. Harsh and strict punishments will go to any poacher who kills and sells British animal products abroad and those who severely hurt or kill a protected animal of Britain.

The complete isolationism of the state's foreign policy will enable Britain to embark on the annexation of Antarctica and Greenland for resources and freely attack the Islamic State and other Islamic terrorist groups in the Middle East. Britain will become a free state, not monitored by the United Nations, the NATO alliance or the European Union. The British government will have complete control over national affairs, just how it should be; under an extremely decisive government which gets things done quickly which is loyal to this Distributist ideology. The impending inevitable World Wars will henceforth be dodged, and Britain could seize this opportunity to gain the Arctic colonies while the UN is ineffective and busy.

The formidable military will employ millions of men, keeping them busy and prepared for anything. Advanced radar sensors will detect any approaching vehicle or missile to Britain's shores, accurately concluding whether it is a unwanted foreign object. With a military as advanced and as large as Britain's under a Distributist government, no major world power will dare invade Britain. Millions from around the world will travel to the UK to spectate the vastly different way of life in Britain, thousands or millions of poor people from foreign countries will attempt to immigrate to Britain. The ones that are granted British citizenship will have to fully integrate into British culture. The government will take advantage of the increased tourism by claiming a valuable item off each tourist (which would be distributed in the markets) in return of their legal access to the country for a limited amount of time and a safe passage home.

Employment levels will rise rapidly as the government will have control of young people's lives post-education and thus able to control the sectors of jobs and distribute the best people more accurately in their areas of strength. People will also live in fear of the thought of being humiliated under Class 4 unemployed status as well as the harsh lifestyle experienced under Class 4 for all people. In times of desperate need the Distributist government can take advantage of their control of the workforce. For instance, if there isn't enough vegetables and corn produced, then the government can focus agricultural workers to focus on vegetable and corn production in the vertical farms. In war, also the government can focus on the production of firearms, armour, aircraft and armoured vehicles much more efficiently.

With the colonies of Antarctica and Greenland, national production rates will soar, their large size's with their resources will be the crown jewel of the new British Empire. Industrial workers will be monitored by state officials and each individual will be required to achieve a daily target output. At the end of the working day, state officials will monitor the quality of the produce to ensure that produce quality is reasonably good and it's quantity is fine. Strict physical punishments will be enforced on industrial workers who fail to meet requirements, in this way industrial workers will work harder and focus more to deliver enough produce and a good enough refinement to the product. Other workers in different sectors of work who underperform should be sacked and replaced with a more hard-working individual.

Society will be much more open and acceptable of different people's opinions and belief's with the exception of Islam. For the first time, Cathedrals and other places of worship will be enlarged and be the place of worship of a number of different beliefs which are not necessarily religious, such as Darwinism, Buddhism, Spiritualism, Paganism and Atheism. Open sexual activities between strangers will be widespread and encouraged, in an effort to bond and unite people, tending to the needs of frustrated men and making people happier. In this sense, Britain will be more united and free than ever before, happier and open to different interpretations.

Overall, I conclude that the Distributist regime will ultimately be the pinnacle of Human politics. It will spark a new era for the Human race and will be the saviour of Humanity regarding the inevitable nuclear war, global famine and an AI Revolution. Britain will take full use of her resources, controlling the population to stabilise the country. Replacing a traditional Capitalist economy centralised on currency, the needs of the people will be met by means of the government distribution of resources and production. If something disastrous happens, then the government could restrict the population in order to achieve the needs promised to all four classes. If production quality of quantity doesn't meet requirements, then more focus on employing people in the industrial sector should be implemented through the government control of people's future post-education. Once the Muslims are tossed out of the country and Greenland and Antarctica are colonised, then the population could probably be increased to 100 million. Britain will become a superpower again through Antarctica and Greenland's resources, an increase in population and a focus on militarism.

After probably centuries of struggle for British Rulership, the English-speaking states will transform the British Empire into the first hyperpower, and the most powerful nation in the world by a considerable margin; especially if a devastating war occurs before the English-speaking states are implemented into the British Empire.

The Distributist regime will help the capable unemployed people in the present seeking work, guaranteeing them a job in the process. At the same time, the ones who are unemployed because they don't want to work will be living in notably worse conditions than now. This is especially true for the unemployed families or mothers with multiple children and newly arrived immigrants who get more than what they need and deserve at this point in time. The social gap between the rich and the poor, in the Distributist sense of Class 1 compared to Class 3, will be reduced. Murderers will be punished in accordance to their victim's relations and religious extremism will be eliminated as a generation upon generation grow up listening and accepting other people's belief's and views. Overall, having summarising all these advantages, my political views are superior to the present system in every way.

www.ingramcontent.com/pod-product-compliance
Lightning Source LLC
Chambersburg PA
CBHW072222170526
45158CB00002BA/709